Lands and Peoples of the World

It is a volume of Travels and Observations;
wherein are described the situation,
polity, and customs of various nations.

Thomas Shaw (1694–1751)

CURTIS INTERNATIONAL/LIBRARY OF KNOWLEDGE

An astronaut's view of India and Ceylon. Photo taken from a height of nearly 500 miles by Charles Conrad and Richard Gordon from Gemini XI.

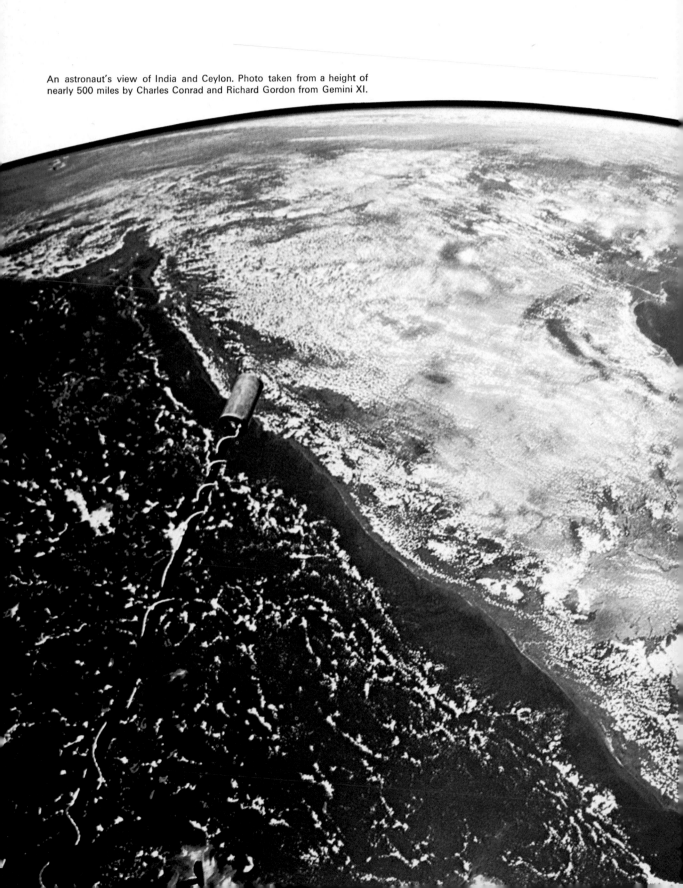

LANDS
AND
PEOPLES
OF THE
WORLD

AN ALDUS BOOK

CURTIS BOOKS
A division of
The Curtis Publishing Company
Philadelphia • New York

© **ALDUS BOOKS LIMITED, London 1968.**

Relief maps © Geographical Projects, a division
of Aldus Books.
First printing. All rights reserved,
including without limitation the right to reproduce
this book or portions thereof in any form.
Printed in Germany by Mohndruck, Gütersloh.
Library of Congress Catalog   No 68–26186

PETER FINCH   Executive editor
                Aldus Books, London
ROBERT E. BURT   Production editor
ELIZABETH MacCALLUM   Editor
ROSEMARY DAVIES   Senior assistant editor
LUCIA STANIELS   Assistant editor
ANN CRAIG   Assistant editor
GUENTER RADTKE   Art director
CORNELIUS CARDEW   Art editor

Introduction by Sir Julian Huxley F. R. S.

This is the first of a series of 18 volumes surveying the whole vast field of human knowledge and experience from the earliest times to the present day. It has been specially prepared by an international team of editors, writers, designers and researchers for family reading throughout North America. My own task in guiding the series has been made easier by a panel of distinguished American and Canadian scholars.

In planning the series we had a much more ambitious aim than the creation of just another set of reference books. We wanted to bring flesh and color to the bare bones of fact, to explain and describe in a way that A through Z treatment would never permit.

Freedom from the constrictions of the conventional alphabetic encyclopedia brings many advantages. There is more scope for concepts and ideas to stir the imagination and stimulate the mind. The more relaxed approach makes it easier to show that knowledge can be fun. Each major subject can be treated as an integrated whole, with its themes logically arranged and developed, and can be given the proper perspective in its world setting. This last is particularly important now that we live in a world of instant communication, with everyone and everywhere just around the corner.

So in this series you will find that each major field of knowledge has its own volume or volumes. For example, LANDS AND PEOPLES OF THE WORLD is one of two volumes devoted to Geography. History has three volumes, Technology two, and so on.

At the same time we have not overlooked the importance of quick reference. The final volume is more than an index to the whole series; each entry begins with basic facts about the subject, making the volume virtually a concise encyclopedia in itself.

We have been concerned as much with looking as with reading. Each volume is generously illustrated with lavish use of color.

Every book is in a sense a travel book, part of a journey in search of knowledge. Here, then, are the first chapters in such a journey. With my colleagues in this project, I hope that you will find them satisfying and rewarding.

Julian Huxley

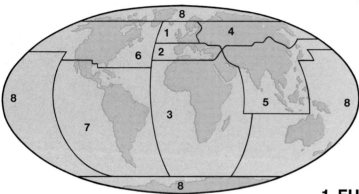

The numbers on this globe refer to the different regions, as listed in the table of contents.

CONTENTS

This book is about the world, its people, where they live, how they live, and their changing relationships with their environment. Jet-age communications have drawn remote areas closer than ever before, and so there is a greater need to know more about other parts of the world than our own. Here we have divided the world into a number of regions, and look at the characteristics of each.

The World

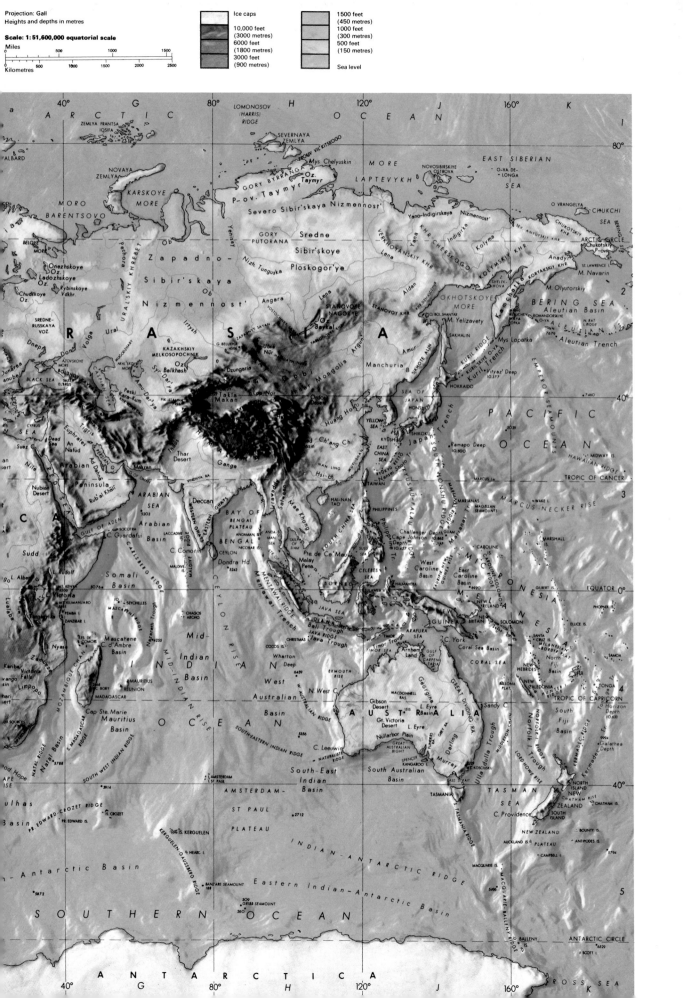

At the western end of the Caledonian mountain system is Ben Nevis, the highest peak in the whole of the British Isles, seen here from the Corpach shore of Loch Linnhe below Fort William, Inverness-shire. Though the mountain is a formidable test of climbing skill, especially in winter, there is a road leading to the top for those who like to mountaineer in comfort.

1

EUROPE: THE NORTHWEST

Northwest Europe, a region of cool summers and mild winters, varied soils, valuable mineral resources and highly developed industries, is densely populated. As Mediterranean influence began to decline about 500 years ago, leadership in ideas, power and material progress became centered in Northwest Europe, which provided the daring and enterprise that pioneered new sea routes and opened up new continents.

British Isles and Scandinavia

A broken chain of very old mountains (formed about 400 million years ago) stretches from Ireland and Scotland along the northwestern seaboard of Scandinavia. These mountains are called the Caledonian System after Caledonia, the ancient name of Scotland. Lowlands lie south and east of this mountain chain, but those in Britain are very different from the lowlands in Scandinavia.

The British lowlands are made of rocks that are much younger than the mountains and these lowland rocks lie in alternating hard and soft layers. So there is a special kind of landscape: low hills with one steep slope *(scarp)* and one gentle slope *(dip)* where the hard beds reach the surface, and valleys where rivers wore away the soft rocks.

In Scandinavia the lowland rocks form the Baltic Shield (a little like the Canadian Shield in eastern Canada), millions of years older than the Caledonian highlands; so very old that they have worn away until they are almost flat. They slope gently southeast to form the Scandinavian lowlands.

Since its formation the Caledonian System has been fractured by successive waves of earth movements and worn down by the forces of erosion. Only the hardest rocks, like granite, gneiss and quartzite, are left. Streams can only cut their valleys along fractures and *faults,* lines of weakness in the rocks.

British Isles and Scandinavia

Left: a sketchmap illustrating the major physical divisions. The maximum extent of Ice Age glaciation is indicated by the gray wash covering Iceland, northern Germany and most of England, and by dark brown on young mountains.

Left below: Hekla, one of several volcanoes in the snow-covered area of Iceland, shown here during the 1947 eruption. Ash and lava were thrown nearly twenty miles into the air. Below: a chalk escarpment of the Downs, which run across southern England.

The spectacular scenery in the mountains of Northwest Europe is a result of the Ice Age. A million years ago ice covered Scandinavia, Iceland and nearly all of the British Isles. Glaciers moved down from the mountains along river courses and gouged out tremendously deep U-shaped valleys. 20,000 years ago the ice began to retreat. Water from melting ice made the sea level rise about 300 feet, drowning the coastline and flooding coastal valleys to form long, narrow inlets like the fiords of Norway and the sea lochs of Scotland. Melting glaciers produced rivers in the steep-sided valleys; and small tributary glaciers gave rise to the streams that cascade down to join the main rivers.

In some parts of Sweden and Finland the ice swept the surface clean and exposed bare rock. When the ice melted, the water washed out huge quantities of debris and deposited it as low ridges (*moraines*) or evenly, as *glacial drift*, on the North European Plain. Lakes formed where glaciers had scoured holes in the rocks or where moraines dammed streams.

Iceland is only 60 million years old, a youngster

by the geological calendar. The island is made up almost entirely of volcanic rocks and has many active volcanoes. Along with the volcanoes there are geysers and also hot springs from which the capital, Reykjavik, gets its hot water. A lot of the island is desolate or under snow; the whole population lives in a quarter of the country's area.

Iceland and Northwest Europe are warmed in winter by the North Atlantic Drift, part of the Gulf Stream, which comes across the Atlantic from off the Florida coast. Norway's ports are ice-free all winter and even at latitude 71°N the sea never freezes; while the St Lawrence River in North America, which is less than 50°N, freezes over for four months in winter.

Prevailing onshore westerly winds pass over the warm water of the Gulf Stream and pick up a lot of water vapor. Annual rainfall at Bergen on the west coast of Norway is 80 inches and at Stockholm is 22 inches. In eastern Sweden and Finland summer days are very long because the region is so far north. At the Arctic Circle on June 21st the sun never sets and on December 21st the sun never rises.

Norwegian fiords, like this one near Gudvangen, were probably formed by earth movements which caused great cracks in the mountains. But their final impressive shaping is due almost entirely to glacial movement during the Ice Age.

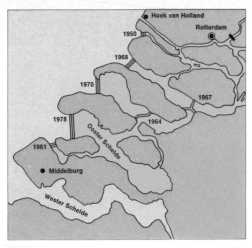

Hills and Plains of Northern Europe

The Delta Plan will free the southwest Netherlands from flood dangers and win land from the sea. The new dykes convert the present tidal area into a lake and make possible new highways linking districts previously dependent on water transport.

▭▭▭ Main closing dikes
▭▭▭ Secondary dikes
▬▬ Adjustable flood barriers

Winter in Holland. Such scenes are rare in Northwest Europe except towards the interior of the continent away from the warming influence of the Gulf Stream.

The hills and plains of northern Europe, across the Baltic Sea from Scandinavia, form three east-west bands: the southern uplands and scarplands, the central highlands and the North European Plain. The River Rhine, Europe's great water highway, flows north from Switzerland across these areas.

In southern Germany the Rhine runs through a *rift valley* between the Vosges Mountains and the Black Forest. Rift valleys formed when a rock mass cracked on four sides and the middle sank. The Rhine valley has some of the most fertile soils in Germany. The scarplands, which are also good farm land, lie east of the Black Mountains. Both areas are dry and warm enough for grapes to ripen; and their wines are famous.

The central uplands are made of old, worn rocks which pushed up as low, stumpy mountains. The Rhine cuts through in a magnificent gorge between Bingen and Bonn. Heaped against the mountains is *loess*, which makes extremely fertile soil. Loess forms from fine silt particles which blew south when the ice sheets retreated.

The wedge-shaped North European Plain stretches from its narrow end in Belgium, where the Ardennes Mountains come down to within 100 miles of the sea, more than 2,000 miles northeast to the Ural Mountains in Russia. The Plain is generally flat, masked by glacial drift, with slight hills and ridges of morainic material a few hundred feet high. Soils are sandy and produce wide stretches of heathland with pine and birch trees. Farmers can only cultivate this land by using huge quantities of chemical fertilizers. But there are some patches of fertile soil—for example, along the alluvial plains of river valleys. In parts of Germany and Poland, rivers zigzag across the Plain where glaciers diverted them from north-south to east-west channels. Linking canals cut across some of the broad, swampy U-shaped valleys between the rivers. These rivers empty into the North Sea and the Baltic Sea. Along the North Sea coast there are many sandy islands,

formed when the incessant action of the sea and the wind broke up sand dunes. The Baltic coast is smooth, with islands only on the western side.

In Belgium and the Netherlands, the Rhine, Meuse and Scheldt are slow, meandering streams which have built up huge deltas of silt and alluvium. A lot of land between these rivers is only just above sea level and floods easily. For hundreds of years the Dutch have been reclaiming this land. First they build dikes to keep out the water and then they pump the land dry. Afterwards the soil is fertilized to eliminate acidity and salt. Now the Dutch are draining land that was once under water: Their largest project is the drainage of the Zuider Zee. They built a dike cutting the Zuider Zee off from

The Rhine, the busiest and longest water highway in western Europe, is navigable by large barges from Basle to the North Sea. Vineyards (right) cover the steep walls of the Rhine Gorge and though most of the buildings hug the edge of the river, roads and railways run along the valley bottom.

the North Sea to form a fresh-water lake, Ijssel Meer. Then they built other dikes enclosing smaller areas and pumped these dry.

Climatically the hills and plains of northern Europe can be divided in half. The Gulf Stream warms the north and west. Belgium, the Netherlands and Northwest Germany have mild winters and cool summers. Annual rainfall amounts to between 25–35 inches. Farther south and east the climate is less maritime. Summers are hotter, winters colder and it is drier. Berlin has an annual rainfall of 23 inches, most in summer. Although total rainfall is small in the east, winter snow may lie on the ground for weeks and rivers freeze over, while in Belgium this is rare.

Luneburg Heath, north Germany, a low sandy ridge between the Aller and Elbe Rivers covered with heather and scrub where farming is difficult. Large areas of the heath are now used as tank training grounds by the armies of NATO.

The Mer de Glace, a 3½-mile long glacier on the northern slopes of Mont Blanc in the French Alps near Chamonix. The striping across the glacier shows the direction in which the ice is moving; the points on the chevrons being towards the melting point which is the source of the river Arveyron flowing to the right.

The Alpine Countries and France

The Alps, one of Europe's major mountain ranges, curve east from the Mediterranean Sea to the river Danube, with hundreds of peaks over 10,000 feet high and the biggest glaciers on mainland Europe.

Austria, about two thirds the size of New York State, is at the northeastern end of this arc. It is a mountainous country with snow, glaciers and pretty mountain villages. The Austrian Alps are less than 10,000 feet high, much lower than the mountains of Switzerland. Valleys are longer, wider and easier to travel along than those in the Swiss Alps. The only lowland areas are in the east along the Danube valley and in the fertile Vienna Basin between the Alps and Carpathian Mountains. Here Vienna, once capital of the powerful Austro-Hungarian Empire, is now a center for trade, banking and commerce, a route focus and linking point between east and west Europe.

People often think there are nothing but mountains in Switzerland too, but only just over half of the country is alpine. The Swiss Alps reach 13,000–15,000 feet. Alpine valleys are deep and U-shaped. Forests, usually fir and pine, cover the valley sides. In summer herdsmen take their flocks to graze on highland pastures above the forests.

Most Swiss live on the relatively flat Central Plateau, or Alpine Foreland, north of the Alps. The plateau is about 1,300 feet high south of the Jura Mountains, but rises to 4,600 feet near the Alps. Part is forested but there is considerable pasture and crop land and the whole area is patterned with rivers and lakes. The Jura Mountains lie north of the Central Plateau. Formed of limestone, they are a good example of *fold mountains* and look like a tightly folded sheet of corrugated steel.

Curving down into southeast France, the Alps form one of the five highland regions of this country. These regions lie like spots on a domino and between them are lowland basins bordering the sea.

In the south, the Rhône flows down to the Mediterranean through a broadening funnel of lowland, the shape of an inverted Y. North of this, between the Central Plateau on the west and the Alps on the east, the Rhône-Saône corridor forms one of the lowland routeways linking two areas with different climates and products—north and south Europe.

The Aquitaine Basin borders the Bay of Biscay. Here it is warm enough for grapes to ripen, since summer temperatures average 70°F and winter, 40–50°F.

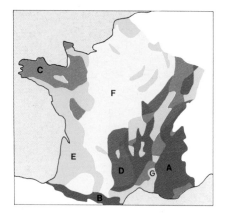

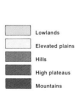

Lowlands

Elevated plains

Hills

High plateaus

Mountains

A Alps and Juras   B The Pyrenees
C Northwest Peninsula   D Central Plateau
E Aquitaine Basin   F Paris Basin   G Rhône

In the north lies the Paris Basin, like a shallow stack of saucers that get broader the deeper they are. The lowest layer is limestone, then come clay, limestone, clay; and the surface layer is chalk with patchy deposits of alluvium, silt and loess. Erosion has worn away the softer beds so the harder ones stand out like ribs around the Basin making a series of gently curving scarps, which are especially well formed southeast of Paris. Clay valleys lie between the scarps. The French call the porous chalk region "Dry Champagne" and the clay valley to the southeast "Wet Champagne". Champagne, the famous French wine, comes from this area.

The Massif Central or Central Plateau is the middle of the "domino". It is about 3,000 feet high and dotted with the broken-down cones of extinct volcanoes (called *puys*) which reach about 5,000 feet. The Pyrenees in the southwest were formed the same time as the Alps. Peninsular Brittany in northwest France is a low plateau with an irregular coastline.

The French Alps have many peaks over 9,000 feet high, including the highest mountain in western Europe, 15,780 foot-high Mont Blanc.

Top: a view of Zermatt with the Matterhorn's jagged peak towering in the background. This scene is like thousands more in Switzerland where the picturesque is carefully and shrewdly preserved because it helps attract the tourists who supply a significant part of the national income.

Below: The Hofburg, Vienna. This old imperial palace recalls the former glories of this ancient city when Vienna was the capital of the Austro-Hungarian Empire and the Hapsburgs ruled. Standing on the south bank of the Danube, Vienna is a cultural and commercial center, a manufacturing and trading city, and a river port.

Agriculture and Fisheries

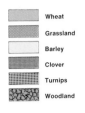
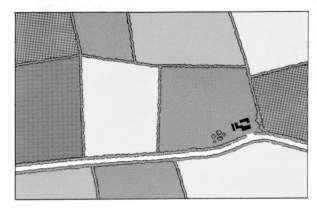

Field plan of a typical Northwest European 400-acre farm which has been divided into 11 fields, most of them under rotation. Barley is the main crop.

Farming in Northwest Europe owes much to the favorable climate of the region. Most of Northwest Europe lies between the 40° and 60° north parallels of latitude. Only Iceland, Finland and Scandinavia fringe the north polar regions. This means that most of the region is free from tropical and polar extremes of climate. Generally the Northwest European climate is moist, warm and stimulating.

Northwest Europe is also fortunate in its wide variety of fertile soils. Some of the richest are in the Aquitaine and Paris Basins, East Anglia and the loess belt bordering the North European Plain. In these areas the farms are large and the yield per acre is usually higher than in the United States because the soil is so fertile and so carefully farmed. Arable farming predominates, with wheat, sugar beet, barley and clover as the main crops. But large areas of the flat English fenlands also grow vegetables, especially potatoes for the national market; and are also known for their flower bulbs and fruit. Bulb growing is also a traditionally famous and important industry in the Netherlands. The Aquitaine summer is warm and dry enough for grapes to ripen well and corn and tobacco crops to thrive.

Denmark and the Netherlands specialize in dairy farming. In these countries cattle can graze nearly

Stacking Swiss cheeses. Switzerland exports cheese to more than 50 countries scattered all over the world. Besides cheese, milk chocolate and condensed milk are exported. The Swiss Plateau north of the Alps is good dairying country.

all year on the good pastures, but grain and root crops are grown for supplementary fodder, especially in Denmark. Hog raising often goes along with dairy farming since hogs can be reared on dairy byproducts like skim milk and whey. Danish butter and bacon, and Dutch cheeses, are famous all over the world.

Along the highland fringes in western Ireland, northwest Britain, Norway, northern Sweden and Finland are small patches of lowland. An average of 30 inches of rain falls annually in these coastal areas, and summers are short. The land is mostly pasture, but hay, barley and root crops are also grown for local supply.

Lowland Ireland has a lot of pasture, and farmers there concentrate on dairy cattle and produce. The air is always moist, the ground dries out slowly after rain and the grass is lush and green all year. This is why Ireland is often called "the Emerald Isle".

The upland soils of Northwest Europe are too thin and poor, and the slopes too steep, for crop growing. The weather is harsh in winter and stock raising is the only kind of farming possible. Sheep, which provide both meat and wool, are raised on highlands where the winters are comparatively mild and there is enough pasture. Large flocks graze on the uplands of Wales, Scotland and northern England, and also on the Pyrenees, the Alps and the Central Plateau of France. In Lapland, in the extreme north of Scandinavia, large herds of reindeer graze on the *tundra*—bleak and almost treeless land where mosses, lichens and other dwarf plants are the only vegetation, and where the subsoil is always frozen. In the uplands of southern Norway farmers keep goats. In Switzerland the mountain pastures are summer grazing grounds.

Farms in Northwest Europe usually have both arable and pasture land. These *mixed farms*, as they are called, have many advantages. An obvious one is that the farmer can feed his animals on the fodder crops he grows and then use the animals' manure to fertilize the land.

Forests cover huge areas of Sweden and Finland,

so forest products form a large part of the manufactures and exports. Nearly all Finland's wealth comes from her forests, which cover almost three quarters of the country's land surface. Thousands of trees, mainly conifers, go every year to make pulp for paper and to feed the sawmills, plywood and hardboard factories.

A typical scene in rural Finland where industry is mainly based on the immense coniferous forests. These extend from the edge of the stunted tundra region in the north to the tall pine forests on the Baltic shores.

Below: Norwegian logs on their way to a pulp mill. Each of these shapes is made up of thousands of tree trunks enclosed by a boom made of chained logs. Norway exports most of her timber as wood-pulp, paper, plywood and cellulose.

The seas of North Europe, especially those round Britain, are shallow—less than 100 fathoms (600 feet) deep—and are breeding and feeding grounds for many kinds of fish. Britain and other countries bordering the North Sea make large catches of herring and other fish in this shallow basin. But the leading fishing country is Norway, whose annual catch is usually greater than that of any other European country except the U.S.S.R. From their inshore waters the Norwegians get cod, herring and brisling. Vestfiord, between the Lofoten Islands and the northern mainland of Norway, is an important winter center for cod fishing. But, like Britain and Germany, Norway sends her fishing vessels much farther afield. Her whaling fleets (Norway controls half the world's whaling industry) sail regularly to the Antarctic. There are virtually no whales now in the Arctic.

Fishing is Iceland's main industry since more than three quarters of this large volcanic island is unproductive and there are few natural resources. Some sheep and cattle are reared and small crops of hay, potatoes and turnips are grown. British trawlers also fish Icelandic waters for cod.

Mineral Resources and Industry

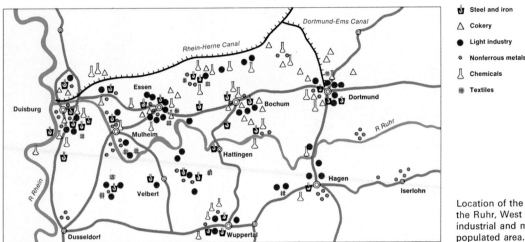

Location of the main industries in the Ruhr, West Germany's chief industrial and most densely populated area.

Northwest Europe was the world's first industrialized area. Power is vital to industry and this region had the great coal reserves to produce that power.

Britain led the way in mining development, and produced 173 million tons of coal in 1966-7; but the best seams were exhausted long ago, and production is rapidly declining. There are coal fields all along the northern margins of the low block mountains in Central Europe—in northeast and central France, Belgium, the Netherlands, the Ruhr, Saxony and Silesia. The Ruhr is Europe's largest coal field and still has resources great enough to last for centuries.

Scandinavia, the Alps and the Pyrenees have no coal but plenty of water, the chief source of hydro-electric power. Scandinavia has developed one third of her potential and Sweden even exports electricity to Denmark by a cable under the narrow strait between the two countries. Nuclear power stations also provide electricity all over Europe; in fact, in many areas it is the cheapest form of electricity.

Southwest France has natural gas which is piped as far away as Paris. Natural gas, which will soon provide one sixth of Britain's total energy requirements, was recently discovered off the British coast under the bed of the North Sea. Most countries import crude oil, but Nottinghamshire (England), the Netherlands and Germany have small petroleum deposits.

Deposits of non-ferrous ores are inadequate in Europe but the continent has good iron ore supplies for iron and steel. Ores containing 20–30% iron are mined in Lorraine, northeast France and in the

east of England. North and central Sweden have better quality ores: more than 60% iron-content.

The chief European source of bauxite, which is used in making aluminium, is in southeast France. Deposits at Les Baux (from which the mineral gets its name) have been worked out; and France now only meets a small part of European needs. Common salt and lignite deposits form the basis of chemical industries in the Leipzig area.

Industrial Northwest Europe falls into two zones, "black" and "white". The black zone, mainly centered on coal fields or where there are raw materials, takes in Britain, Northeast France, Belgium and Germany. These areas are full of coal mines and tips, foundries and factories making all kinds of iron and steel goods. Newer automobile, chemical and electrical industries have developed here too, since they depend on iron and steel production for machinery and raw materials.

The Ruhr coal field is the backbone of German industry, especially heavy industry. Here fifteen industrial towns—all with populations of more than 100,000—as well as many other smaller places, have grown up close together. Good rail and river communications accelerated their growth.

Some areas concentrate on textiles. Lancashire, in England, is famous for cotton goods, Yorkshire for its wool industry. Northeast France makes both wool and cotton goods. Factories in Belgium and Northern Ireland, originally dependent on local flax supplies, manufacture millions of square yards of linen every year. Nearly all textile areas also make synthetic fibers like nylon.

Top: At this hydroelectric power station in central
Sweden the natural force of falling water provides
cheap electric power. The scattered industries of
Scandinavia, Finland and the Alps countries are
almost entirely powered by hydroelectricity. As
these areas have no coal fields this cheap power
has been vital to their development.

The "white" industrial zone is in Scandinavia,
Finland and the Alps. The major power source is
electricity, not coal, so industrial towns are clean
and free from smoking factory chimneys. Using
electricity for iron and steel production is expensive.
But the electrochemical and electrosmelting industries, prominent in the "white" zone, need large
amounts of electricity. There are aluminium factories everywhere as well as smelters making certain
metals for steel alloys. Nitrogen extracted from the
atmosphere forms the basis of a wide variety of
electrochemical products.

Transportation of raw materials and finished
products in the "white" zone is important. Water
transport is easiest and cheapest. So landlocked
Switzerland concentrates on making small high-
value articles like watches and quality electrical
goods.

Products like Swedish glass, Scottish tweeds, Italian leather and Swiss watches show the extremely
high standard of European craftsmanship and skill.
These products remain competitive in a world
market dominated by mass production.

Left: a 1,200-ton mixer furnace at the Spencer
steel works near Newport, Monmouthshire, England. Today Britain is the world's fifth largest steel
producing nation with a net annual delivery
capacity of over 20 million tons of finished steel.

Top: this Swedish girl typifies the fair-haired and blue-eyed people of Scandinavia, north Germany, Denmark and Holland.
Below: in France, the native country of this young girl, more bread is probably eaten than in any other country in the world. These loaves are sometimes over a yard long.

Life in Northwest Europe

Although the continent of Europe is less than half the size of North America, its average population density is five times greater. Its total population is about 444 million, and of these about 220 million live in Northwest Europe—a large population for a comparatively small region. The density of population is especially high in Britain, Belgium, the Netherlands and parts of France and Germany where the growth has been so great that towns and cities have often expanded to join one another in a single large populated area—what Americans called a *megalopolis* and the British a *conurbation*.

These huge urban areas occur particularly in a broad arc running from Liverpool, Manchester and Leeds in England through northern France, Belgium and the Ruhr to southeast Germany. By contrast some other countries, like Norway and Finland, are thinly populated.

Throughout history Northwest Europe has been a region to which migrants have come from the east, many across the North European Plain, the great east-west routeway. Some were drawn by the milder climate and richer farmland of the region, others came to escape fresh waves of invaders from the east. Some braved the North Sea and others ventured even farther, so anticipating the great Age of Discovery and the time when Northeast Europe would become a springboard for fresh migrations to the Americas, Africa and Australasia. Some were fugitives from political or religious oppression.

The recurrent themes in the story of mankind are movement and change. As men wandered, they changed and mingled with others who were themselves moving and changing. This age-old process is now so advanced that we cannot really identify any country by a single physical type, although we can often point to distinctive characteristics. Scandinavians are usually tall and have fair hair and complexions. Southern Europe has its "Mediterranean" peoples, distinguished by their medium height, fine bone structure and dark complexions. The fringe peoples of Northwest Europe—the Welsh, Scots, Irish and Bretons—are often short, dark and stocky and usually speak a Celtic language.

What Times Square is to New York, Piccadilly Circus is to London. The Romans founded London, Britain's capital and leading port, and today roughly a quarter of Britain's total population live in London and the surrounding 40-mile belt of country.

The diversity of languages also reflects the movement of peoples. French, Spanish and Italian have their roots in Latin, the language of the Roman Empire, and its dialects. English, Dutch, Flemish and German are basically related, but English contains many words derived from the Latin through French and at least two, cocoa and tomato, from the Aztec language.

Such diversity has not helped the spread of thought and knowledge in Europe or the growth of understanding between nations. Some countries have language differences to overcome inside their own frontiers. For example, the people of north Belgium are mostly Flemings speaking Flemish, while those of the south are Walloons who speak French. In Switzerland four languages are spoken— German, French, Italian and Romansh.

Sometimes differences between peoples or within countries have been accentuated, or even created by political events. A good example in Europe is the partition of Germany at the end of World War II. This, and the building of the Berlin Wall later, made West Berlin an island of West German territory in Communist East Germany. Another is the division of Ireland. Northern Ireland is a part of the United Kingdom. The south is the independent Republic of Ireland.

Northwest Europe has been developing politically for hundreds of years. Its forms of government include constitutional monarchies like Belgium,

Denmark, the Netherlands, Norway, Sweden and the United Kingdom, where the head of state is a king or queen; and republics like Austria, Finland, France, Ireland, Iceland and West Germany, where the head of state is an elected president.

Material living standards in Northwest Europe are high. Only in North America, Australia and New Zealand are they higher in terms of wealth per person. Most people live in well built houses or apartments, and the symbols of affluent society— cars, vacuum cleaners, refrigerators and washing machines—are found everywhere.

London's Wembley Stadium, which holds 100,000 spectators, is the home of association football. This form of football originated in Britain and is now being popularized in the United States.

Europe

Projection: Azimuthal Equidistant
Heights and depths in metres

Scale: 1:19,500,000

Miles

| 0 | 100 | 200 | 300 | 400 | 500 |

Kilometres

| 0 | 100 | 200 | 300 | 400 | 500 | 600 | 700 | 800 | 900 |

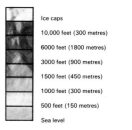

Ice caps
10,000 feet (300 metres)
6000 feet (1800 metres)
3000 feet (900 metres)
1500 feet (450 metres)
1000 feet (300 metres)
500 feet (150 metres)
Sea level

Towns:

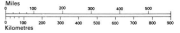

■ over 1,000,000
● over 500,000
● over 250,000
• under 250,000

International boundaries
Boundaries under dispute
Major air routes
Major sea routes

Northwest Europe and the World

There are several reasons why Northwest Europe has become one of the four most densely inhabited regions of the world—its favorable climate and geographical position, its abundance of natural resources and the enterprising ability of its people to make the most of these. The same reasons go far to explain Northwest Europe's importance as a center of world influence and ideas.

Until the discovery of America in 1492, European influence in world affairs centered on the Mediterranean, where western civilization itself had been born. But with the rapid growth of nations across the Atlantic, the balance increasingly shifted to Northwest Europe, to vigorous trading and empire-building nations like Britain, France and the Netherlands. This movement was decisively confirmed by the use Northwest Europeans made of their considerable mineral resources, especially coal and iron ore. Coupled with the energy of hardworking and inventive craftsmen and technicians, these resources made Northwest Europe the world's first great industrial area.

The rapid growth of industry and population soon outstripped agricultural production. Today Northwest Europe imports more than three quarters of its food. Another vital import is petroleum. The Northwest has some oil and natural gas, and is finding more under the North Sea, but the bulk of the requirement has to come in from abroad. In some countries hydroelectricity is an important source of power for home and industry. But while the Northwest imports, it also exports. Few regions can match its output of manufactured goods.

With industrial expansion came the development of transportation and communications. There were immediate natural advantages. Most rivers in Northwest Europe flow north or west to the Atlantic or the North Sea, providing easy inland communication and cheap freight transport. A lot of the region is plains country and, except for the Caledonian System in the north and the Alps in the southeast, there are no impassable mountain ranges. An excellent road, rail, air and waterway network now covers all of Europe.

The importance of overseas trade is reflected in the number of large towns in Northwest Europe that are also ports. Rotterdam and London are the leaders; then come Hamburg and Antwerp. The many busy river or sea ports include Glasgow, Liverpool, Bristol, Marseilles, Bordeaux, Le Havre, Strasbourg, Bremen, Copenhagen, Oslo and Göte-

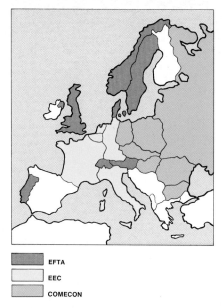

EFTA

EEC

COMECON

Top: the location of Europe's main economic communities. These are: The European Free Trade Association, The European Economic Community, and the Council for Mutual Economic Aid.

Northwest Europe lies at the center of the hemisphere which has the world's great land masses. This central position is of special importance in the age of air travel.

borg. Three quarters of the world's shipping moves in and out of European ports.

After World War II the west European nations moved towards unity. They believed that many post-war economic problems could be solved by abolishing trade barriers. Two separate free trade zones resulted—the European Economic Community (E.E.C.), in which French influence has been considerable, and the European Free Trade Association (E.F.T.A.), which was sponsored by the United Kingdom. Recently some E.F.T.A. countries have been negotiating for membership in the Common Market.

The state opening of Parliament, one of the most colorful pageants associated with Britain's monarchy. Here Queen Elizabeth II is shown at the ceremony in the House of Lords at Westminster Palace, home of the "mother of parliaments". Prince Philip, sits on the Queen's left. On the Queen's right sits Prince Charles, Prince of Wales and heir to the throne. On Prince Philip's left side Princess Anne, the Queen's only daughter.

Western European countries have joined one another and North America in various other co-operative organizations. In 1949 the U.S.A. and Canada joined Western Europe in N.A.T.O. (North Atlantic Treaty Organization), a mutual defense pact against possible Communist aggression. And in 1951 the European Atomic Energy Community was set up to integrate and promote development of nuclear energy for peaceful purposes.

Meanwhile imperialism was retreating. Since World War II the great powers have gradually lost their colonies and in Africa, Asia and elsewhere independent states have emerged. In some cases a special relationship between old imperial power and former colony has been preserved. For example, France maintains associations with many of her former colonies through the sometimes loose links of the French Community. The United Kingdom has closer ties with its former colonies in its Commonwealth of Nations, which takes in a quarter of the world's population.

The tradition of European genius in literature and music, art and science remains as strong as ever. Europe is still the focus of western culture; scientists and technicians are making important contributions in research and industrial development. But in world affairs generally European influence has been overshadowed and diminished by North America and the Soviet Union. Their size and wealth of natural resources alone are sufficient to make them pre-eminent, although no one can afford to ignore Europe's role in world politics.

COUNTRIES OF NORTHWEST EUROPE

ANDORRA
Co-principality
S.W. Europe
Area: 190 sq.miles

Pop: 14,000. **Land use %:** negligible. **Occupations:** mining (iron, alum and lead), quarrying (granite, marble), agriculture (potatoes, grain and tobacco), tourism. **Capital:** Andorra la Vella (2,200).

AUSTRIA*
Republic
Central Europe
Area: 32,000 sq. miles

Pop: 7,290,000. **Land use %:** cultivated 22; meadow and pasture 28; forest 37; waste 13. **Occupations:** agriculture and forestry; manufacturing; commerce and professions. **Industries:** heavy industry (iron and steel), fertilizers, paper, motor vehicles; hydro-electric power. **Capital:** Vienna (1,700,000).

BELGIUM*
Kingdom
N.W. Europe
Area: 12,000 sq. miles

Pop: 9,528,000. **Land use %:** arable and orchard 34; meadow and pasture 25; waste 23; forest and woodland 18. **Occupations:** manufacturing, agriculture, forestry and fishing, commerce, public services. **Industries:** coal, steel and metal products, textiles, glass and chemicals. **Capital:** Brussels (1,066,000).

DENMARK*
Kingdom
N.W. Europe
Area: 17,000 sq. miles

Pop: 4,797,000. **Land use %:** cultivated 63; waste 18; meadow and pasture 11; forest 8. **Occupations:** manufacturing, agriculture, forestry and fishing, public services, commerce. **Industries:** iron and steel, shipbuilding, wool and cotton textiles, chemicals (phosphates). **Capital:** Copenhagen (1,378,000). **Outlying territories** (parts of the kingdom): The Faroe Islands (Area: 540 sq. miles. Pop: 35,000) and Greenland (Area: 840,000 sq. miles. Pop: 34,000).

FINLAND*
Republic
N. Europe
Area: 130,000 sq. miles

Pop: 4,651,000. **Land use %:** forest and woodland 37; meadow and pasture 28; cultivated 22; waste 13. **Occupations:** agriculture and forestry, manufacturing. **Industries:** wood pulp and paper, iron and steel, engineering. **Capital:** Helsinki (679,000).

FRANCE*
Republic
N.W. Europe
Area: 213,000 sq. miles

Pop: 46,100,000. **Land use %:** cultivated 38; meadow and pasture 22; forest and woodland 21; waste 19. **Occupations:** agriculture, forestry and fishing, manufacturing, services, commerce. **Industries:** iron and steel (ships, locomotives, automobiles), aircraft, textiles, chemicals, natural gas, wines and spirits. **Capital:** Paris (7,369,000), **Overseas departments:** Martinique, Guadeloupe, Réunion, Guiana. **Overseas Territories:** French Polynesia, New Caledonia, French Somaliland, Comoro Archipelago, Saint Pierre and Miquelon. Southern and Antarctic Territories, Wallis and Futuna Islands. **Member states of the French Community:** the French Republic, Central African Republic, the Republics of Congo, Gabon, Madagascar, Senegal, Chad. In addition France has 'special relations' with the following republics: Ivory Coast, Dahomey, Upper Volta, Mauritania, Niger, Cameroun; and co-operation agreements with Mali, Togo. **Anglo-French Condominium:** New Hebrides.

GERMANY (WEST)
Federal Republic
N. Europe
Area: 96,000 sq. miles

Pop: 59,793,000. **Land use %:** cultivated 35; forest 29; meadow and grassland 23; waste 13. **Occupations:** manufacturing, public administration, trade and commerce, building, transport. **Industries:** iron and steel, motor vehicles, chemicals, textiles, machinery and scientific instruments. **Capital:** Bonn (141,000).

LAND (STATE)	AREA (sq. miles)	POPULATION	CAPITAL
Baden-Württemburg	13,942	8,534,000	Stuttgart
Bavaria	27,239	10,217,000	Munich
Berlin (West)	186	2,185,000	—
Bremen	156	750,000	—
Hamburg	288	1,847,000	—
Hesse	8,150	5,240,000	Wiesbaden
Lower Saxony	18,290	6,967,000	Hanover
North Rhine-Westphalia	13,157	16,835,000	Düsseldorf
Rhineland-Palatinate	7,665	3,613,000	Mainz
Saarland	991	1,132,000	Saarbrücken
Schleswig-Holstein	6,045	2,473,000	Kiel

ICELAND*
Republic
N. Atlantic Island
Area: 40,000 sq. miles

Pop: 196,000. **Land use %:** waste 79; meadow and pasture 19; cultivated 1; forest and woodland 1. **Occupations:** fishing and seasonal agriculture. **Industries:** fish curing and canning. **Capital:** Reykjavik (78,000).

1 ANDORRA
2 AUSTRIA
3 BELGIUM
4 DENMARK
5 FINLAND
6 FRANCE
7 GERMANY (WEST)
8 ICELAND
9 IRISH REPUBLIC
10 LIECHTENSTEIN
11 LUXEMBOURG
12 NETHERLANDS (HOLLAND)
13 NORWAY
14 SWEDEN
15 SWITZERLAND
16 UNITED KINGDOM OF GREAT BRITAIN
AND NORTHERN IRELAND

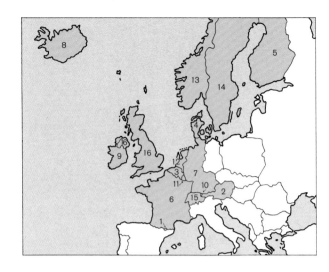

IRISH REPUBLIC*
Republic
N.W. Europe
Area: 27,000 sq. miles

Pop: 2,881,000. **Land use %:** meadow and grassland 48; waste 31; cultivated 19; forest and woodland 2. **Occupations:** agriculture and fishing, services, manufacturing, commerce. **Industries:** textiles, food processing, footwear. **Capital:** Dublin (569,000).

LIECHTENSTEIN
Principality
Central Europe
Area: 61 sq. miles

Pop: 20,000. **Land use %:** meadow and pasture 37; cultivated 25; forest 19; waste 19. **Occupations:** agriculture, tourism. **Industries:** wood and textiles. **Capital:** Vaduz (4,000).

LUXEMBOURG*
Grand Duchy
W. Europe
Area: 1000 sq. miles

Pop: 335,000. **Land use %:** meadow and pasture 38; cultivated 25; waste 19; forest and woodland 18. **Occupations:** manufacturing, agriculture and forestry, commerce and transport. **Industries:** iron and steel, engineering, textiles, chemicals. **Capital:** Luxembourg (79,000).

NETHERLANDS*
Kingdom
N. Europe
Area: 16,000 sq. miles

Pop: 12,573,000. **Land use %:** meadow and pasture 37; cultivated 30; waste 26; forest and woodland 7. **Occupations:** manufacturing, agriculture and fishing, public services, commerce. **Industries:** engineering, ship building, iron and steel, electrical and electronic equipment, textiles, glass, chemicals, processing foodstuffs. **Capital:** Amsterdam (862,000). **Seat of government:** The Hague. **Overseas parts of the kingdom:** Surinam, The Netherlands Antilles.

NORWAY*
Kingdom
N.W. Europe
Area: 125,000 sq. miles

Pop: 3,753,000. **Land use %:** wasteland 74; forest 23; meadow and pasture 1; cultivated 2. **Occupations:** manufacturing, agriculture, forestry, fishing. **Industries:** wood and paper, fish canning, mineral refining, textiles, hydroelectric power. **Capital:** Oslo (483,000).

SWEDEN*
Kingdom
N. Europe
Area: 173,000 sq. miles

Pop: 7,845,000. **Land use %:** forest and woodland 51; waste 38; cultivated 9; meadow and pasture 2. **Occupations:** industry, agriculture, commerce. **Industries:** iron and steel, wood pulp and paper, textiles, hydroelectric power. **Capital:** Stockholm (779,000).

SWITZERLAND
Federal Republic
Central Europe
Area: 16,000 sq. miles

Pop: 5,999,000. **Land use %:** meadow and pasture 41; forest 24; waste 23; cultivated 12. **Occupations:** manufacturing, agriculture and forestry, commerce. **Industries:** engineering, clothing and textiles, watchmaking, foodstuffs, chemicals, wood products. **Capital:** Berne (171,000).

UNITED KINGDOM OF GREAT BRITAIN AND NORTHERN IRELAND* †
Kingdom
N.W. Europe
Area: 94,000 sq. miles

Pop: 54,744,000. **Land use %:** meadow and pasture 49; cultivated 30; waste 14; forest and woodland 7. **Occupations:** manufacturing, public services, commerce, transport. **Industries:** iron and steel, automobiles, aircraft, shipbuilding, engineering, electrical products, atomic power, textiles, chemicals, pottery and glass, etc. **Capital:** London (7,913,000). **Members of the Commonwealth:** United Kingdom, Canada, Australia, New Zealand, India, Pakistan, Ceylon, Ghana, Nigeria, Cyprus, Sierra Leone, Jamaica, Trinidad and Tobago, Uganda, Kenya, Malaysia, Tanzania, Malawi, Malta, Zambia, The Gambia, Singapore, Guyana, Botswana, Lesotho, Barbados, Nauru and Mauritius; and their dependent territories. **Associated States:** Antigua, St. Christopher-Nevis-Anguilla, Dominica, Grenada, St. Lucia. **Colonies, Protectorates and Protected States:** Rhodesia, Swaziland, Brunei, Hong Kong, British Indian Ocean Territory, Seychelles, Gibraltar, Falkland Islands, St. Helena, Bahamas, Bermuda, British Honduras, British Virgin Islands, Cayman Islands, Turks and Caicos Islands, Montserrat, St. Vincent, Fiji, Pitcairn, Tonga, British Solomon Islands, Gilbert and Ellice Islands, New Hebrides (Anglo-French Condominium), British Antarctic Territory.

* Member of the United Nations
† Member of the British Commonwealth

THE MEDITERRANEAN

The almost landlocked Mediterranean has always been a sea highway for the countries around it. Throughout history there have been many links between the peoples of southern Europe and North Africa. The bordering lands are varied, but all are in some sense "Mediterranean", for all of them touch the same sea and often share climate, vegetation and patterns of life.

Peninsulas, Islands and Seas

The Mediterranean Sea, deep and tideless, has only one natural outlet to open ocean, the Strait of Gibraltar at its western end between the Iberian Peninsula and North Africa. About 10 miles wide, the strait links the Mediterranean with the Atlantic. The northeastern outlet, the long and narrow Dardanelles, leads only to the Sea of Marmara and from there by the Bosporus to the Black Sea, a dead end except for the river highways of the U.S.S.R. At the southeast corner of the Mediterranean is a manmade outlet. The Suez Canal cuts across 101 miles of level desert to the Red Sea, providing a route to India and the Far East.

The Sicilian Narrows, between western Sicily and Cape Bon in Tunisia, divide the Mediterranean into two basins. The eastern, which contains the Adriatic, Aegean and other seas, is the larger of the two. The whole Mediterranean is almost penned in by mountain chains. Much of the region is subject to earthquakes and there are active volcanoes, like Etna, Stromboli and Vesuvius.

The mountains around the irregular northern coast are comparatively young geologically. They were formed about 60 million years ago when sediments deposited by rivers in a much larger sea than the present Mediterranean were slowly crumpled and pushed up. Similar ranges appear in northwest Africa, where the rugged peaks of the Atlas Mountains in Algeria and Morocco reach more than 13,000 feet. But east, the low and solid African plateau drops almost straight into the sea at its edge. Here there are few good harbors. Alexandria, the second city and chief port of the United Arab Republic, stands on the west side of the Nile delta.

The smooth coastlines of Israel, Lebanon and Syria have low plateaus inland. East of these is the flat-floored, steep-sided rift valley through which

Positano, a typical Italian fishing village on the shores of the Gulf of Salerno. The houses are built against the sheer cliff face and most streets are long stairways winding up from shore to cliff-top. This village is one of the most popular Italian tourist centers and offers special attractions to swimmers and aqua-lung divers.

the river Jordan slowly meanders. At the lowest part of the valley the Jordan empties into the Dead Sea, 1,286 feet below sea level. It is so much saltier than ocean water that even the worst swimmers float in it like corks. Israel and Jordan look out on each other across the Dead Sea.

The Turkish coastline is more rugged and in the southeast is bordered by the Taurus Mountains. Turkey in Asia consists of the great plateau of Anatolia (Asia Minor). In Europe Turkey has a small area around the cities of Istanbul and Edirne, and so controls the Bosporus, Sea of Marmara and the Dardanelles.

Greece, like neighboring Albania, is mountainous. The Pindus Mountains, an extension of the Dinaric Alps, run from Albania into Greece and disappear beneath the Aegean Sea in a scatter of islands.

Looking towards Italy across the Adriatic is Yugoslavia. Running parallel with the Dalmatian (Adriatic) coast are the Dinaric Alps. Formed mostly of limestone, they have worn away to rugged plateaus and are much lower than the main Alpine ranges. Water sinks quickly through the porous rock, and the fissured surface is usually dry and barren. Caverns and streams lie underground. But here and there on the plateaus are long, flat-floored basins called *poljes* often covered with comparatively fertile soil. *Karst*, the name geologists use to describe this sort of landscape, is a Yugoslav word.

Italy is probably the most Mediterranean in character of all the countries bordering this sea. It thrusts southeast like a boot about to kick a ball. The Appenine Mountains are the backbone of the boot, and bend around, linking with the great curve of the Alps like a reversed question mark. The ball is the fertile island of Sicily. The Appenines are rugged, with rocky hillsides. Patches of lowland are confined to the coastal areas. So people in southern Italy find it difficult to grow enough food for themselves. But in the north, between the westward curve of the Appenines and the much higher ranges of the Alps is the large, fertile Plain of Lombardy, drained by the river Po and its tributaries. Over the years these rivers have brought down in their flood waters the fine silt that makes the Plain's fertile soil. It is densely populated and eco-

Top: one of the Mediterranean's finest natural harbors is the Bay of Kotor, on the Adriatic in Yugoslavia. Development of the port has been hindered by the high mountains behind.
Right: from its source on the slopes of Mount Hermon to the Dead Sea, the River Jordan flows through part of the remarkable rift valley which extends to East Africa. For two thirds of its course the river runs below sea level.

nomically is the most important region of Italy. Below Ferrara the Po has built a huge delta. On the lagoon at its northern end the ancient city-seaport of Venice stands on a cluster of islands. But the Plain's chief city is Milan, an important commercial, transportation and industrial center, and the second largest city in Italy. Another important industrial and transportation center of the north is Turin.

Spain and Portugal together make up the Iberian Peninsula. Most of this square peninsula is plateau country called the *Meseta*, about 2,000 feet high but with ranges rising to 6,000 feet and more. To the southeast are Spain's highest mountains, the Sierra Nevada, which exceed 11,000 feet and may be snowtipped even in midsummer. Most people in this dry, hot peninsula live in the river valleys and coastal lowlands. Both Spain and Portugal are predominantly agricultural countries, but Catalonia, Oviedo and Bilbao are important industrially.

Agriculture and Climate

Top: a Bedouin tribesman and his camel. Bedouins are nomadic tribal people of the deserts of Arabia, Syria and northern Africa. They are Moslems and their wanderings are determined by the grazing needs of their camels, sheep and goats.
Below: Portuguese workers stripping the cork oak's bark by hand. Portugal produces about 50 per cent of the world's cork.

The narrow ribbon of coastal lands around the Mediterranean Sea have the most characteristically "Mediterranean" climate, the kind of climate that is found in other parts of the world—the southern tip of South Africa, central Chile, California and parts of southern Australia.

In summer the sun shines down from a cloudless blue sky and July temperatures average over 80°F. During the warm, moist winters temperatures of 40°–50°F. are not uncommon. Westerly winds from the Atlantic or off the Mediterranean itself bring in rain, so western high ground is the wettest: northwest Spain, the Apennines, the Dinaric Alps, and the Atlas Mountains in north Africa. Rainfall is less in the south and east. Gibraltar has about 35 inches in a year; Marseilles, 23 inches; Rome, 32 inches. But Malta has only 20 inches; Athens, 15 inches and Alexandria, eight inches. In most Mediterranean countries water is precious. So conservation and irrigation are important. Some countries, like Israel, have spectacularly increased agricultural production by using modern techniques.

The land of the region is mostly difficult to cultivate. There are many steep slopes and only small pockets of lowland. When the rain does come, it is often so torrential that the farmers have to terrace the slopes to stop water from washing away precious topsoil. Crops grown for local use include wheat and corn where winters are wet enough. Rice grows in the Po Valley, the Rhône delta and in southeast Spain; melons in southern Spain and Italy; tomatoes everywhere.

Except in Galicia, in northwest Spain, and the wetter parts of the Alps, Apennines and Dinaric Alps, there are few cattle. So people do not usually eat butter. Farmers concentrate on goat and sheep raising. Goats will graze the poor hillside pastures and forage successfully for themselves in scrub and low bushes. The danger is that they may overgraze, loosening the dry soil which is then washed away by the winter rain. In Mediterranean lands shepherds often take their flocks to the higher pastures in summer because it is cooler and moister there.

What the coconut palm is to the Pacific (p. 154), the olive tree is to the Mediterranean. These knarled, twisted trees have very long roots that can draw on moisture deep below the parched, brown surface. They can live for hundreds of years, regu-

larly producing thousands of fruits resembling small plums. Spain is the leading olive country; the province of Jaén alone has about 32 million trees. Few of the olives harvested are eaten fresh in Mediterranean lands. Most are used to make cooking oil. Eating olives are carefully handpicked, but oil olives are beaten from the trees with long poles and pulped into a paste. This paste is spread on esparto grass mats, which are then put through a hydraulic press to force out the oil. The best oil comes from the first pressing.

Another characteristic tree is the cork oak. This evergreen is remarkable since its outer bark can be stripped off every ten years without damaging the tree, which may go on producing cork for 150 years. The trees are not usually stripped for the first time until they are more than 15 years old. The best cork comes from the third stripping on. Eastern Portugal is famous for its cork oak, but there are also valuable cork oak forests in Algeria and Morocco.

Vineyards on terraced hillsides are another common feature of the Mediterranean landscape. Although vines tend to lose a lot of water because their leaves are large, thin and soft, they compensate by drawing up moisture through their deep roots. Vine roots sometimes push down 20 feet or more into the ground.

Grapes provide wine for both local consumption and export. Mediterranean lands have many famous wines; for example, the sherry of the Jerez district of southern Spain and the port of the Douro valley vineyards of Portugal. In the eastern Mediterranean, where it is drier and more sunny, grapes are also slowly dried in the open to provide raisins, sultanas and currants. Currants, named for Corinth in Greece, are produced by drying small black grapes.

Citrus and other fruits are widely grown. Citrus trees can withstand drought, but farmers usually practice irrigation to produce better quality crops. Sicily is noted for its lemons, Spain for the oranges named after Seville, the historic city on the Guadalquivir River in Andalusia, and Israel for its grapefruit and Jaffa oranges. Other fruits grown for export include Italian peaches and pears, the dried figs for which Turkey has always been known, Israeli avocados and dates from the oases of Libya, southern Tunisia and Algeria.

Top: In Spain carts are used to bring the oranges to a central collecting point. Spanish citrus groves are mainly in the east and south of the country, especially in Valencia.
Below: A Greek bowl, made about 500 B.C. The graceful vine motif is a reminder that the Greeks spread the art of vine-growing.

Mineral Resources and Industry

The French Riviera is one of the Mediterranean's most famous resort coasts. Sheltered by mountains to the north, it has a mild climate, and this has encouraged the growth of tourist centers like Cannes and Nice. Once mainly a millionaires' playground, the Riviera now attracts people from all income levels.

Because they do not have many mineral resources most Mediterranean lands are not highly industrialized. Mineral wealth is usually found in old rocks where the deposits have been built up over a long period of time. The mountains of the Mediterranean region are geologically young, so mineral resources are generally poor. The only abundant and widespread "raw material" for industry is cheap labor.

Power has also been a problem. Coal deposits are small and there was little petroleum in the region until the discovery and development of the important new oil fields in Algeria and Libya. Hydroelectric power on a large scale could only be developed in mountain districts with plenty of melting ice and snow to keep the rivers flowing even in summer. Northern Italy and France make great use of such power, and rivers in Spain, Portugal and southern Italy are being harnessed with dams and power stations. Yugoslavia, Greece and Turkey have some hydroelectric power, but the rugged mountains in these countries are not so high as the Alpine systems of the west Mediterranean. The rivers are shorter and there is less rain.

Italy and Spain are the only Mediterranean countries with large-scale industry. Italy's great industrial area lies in the north. The early growth of cities in this area, like Venice, Milan and Turin, was based on routes and trade. Later readily available cheap labor, and coal imported through seaports conveniently close by, encouraged industrial development. Further expansion occurred with the transmission of hydro-electricity from the Alps. Factories now also use natural gas for power.

In this part of Italy the medieval silk industry has grown into the manufacture of all kinds of textiles, from silk to manmade fibers. Factories turn out machines and all kinds of electrical equipment. There are also important chemical plants; and many airplane and automobile factories.

The chemical industry figures prominently in

Florence, the cradle of the Italian Renaissance, is still a treasure house of churches, palaces and art galleries. The city grew up on the Arno River, where it could control trans-Apennine and east-west routes. Many of its priceless art treasures were damaged during the floods of 1966.

another part of Italy—the island of Sicily. Here, mostly on the coastal strip between Augusta and Syracuse, recent industrial development includes an oil refinery and a chemical plant which makes fertilizers from the island's sulfur and potash.

The barren Spanish plateau, where the rocks are older than in most parts of the Mediterranean, has a long history of mining. Its deposits include copper, tin, lead, silver and zinc, and there is even some coal. But Spain's chief coal field is in the north near Oviedo. This coal, with iron ore from the Cantabrian Mountains, is used in the iron and steel plants and engineering plants in Oviedo and Bilbao.

Right: the Fiat automobile plant, Turin. This is the biggest plant of its kind in Italy and the second biggest in Europe. Standing at the junction of the Po and Dora Riparia, Turin is the chief city of Piedmont and fourth city in Italy, coming after Rome, Milan and Naples. Its industries include engineering, textiles and chemicals.

Below: a fine 15th-century plate from the glassmakers of Murano, an island suburb of Venice famous for its glassware since the 13th century. Optical as well as ornamental glass of the first quality is now made there.

Right: the barren Kédia d'Idjil Mountains of Mauritania, northwest Africa (right), have one of the world's richest iron ore deposits. From here a 400-mile long railroad crosses the desert taking the ore from Fort Gouraud to Port Etienne on the coast for shipment.

Barcelona, Spain's second largest city and chief seaport, has become an important industrial center in spite of the absence of local coal and raw materials. Its industries include textiles (especially cotton), machinery, glass, chemicals and food processing. Cables carry hydroelectric power from the Pyrenees 50 or 100 miles to the city.

Both Spain and Italy have important mercury deposits. Bauxite is mined in Italy, Yugoslavia and Greece. Yugoslavia has a wide variety of mineral resources, from coal, iron ore, manganese and lead-zinc ore to the precious metals, gold and silver. Most of her industry is located in the northwest of the country. Turkey is one of the world's chief producers of chrome.

One of the Mediterranean's major industries is tourism. The "raw materials" are sunshine and scenery. In summer tourists crowd the shores of southern Europe. Tourism is highly organized and attracts heavy investment in new hotels, villas and motels. The tourists come mostly from the cooler densely populated countries of northwest Europe. Among the most popular resorts are the Costa Brava and Balearic Islands of Spain, the French and Italian Rivieras, the Adriatic coasts of Italy and Yugoslavia, and the islands of Greece.

Life in Mediterranean Lands

Jerusalem, a city holy to Jews, Christians and Moslems, has been besieged and fought over many times in its long history. In recent years a part of Jerusalem was held by Jordan, but during the brief war of 1967 Israel quickly won control of the whole city.

Compared to North America and Northwest Europe, living standards in lands around the Mediterranean Sea are very low, although they are higher than in Asia. Only northern Italy approaches the living conditions and prosperity of Northwest Europe; but this area is hardly Mediterranean, with its strong industrial bias and urbanization. Everywhere else—through southern Italy, Sicily, Spain, Portugal, Greece, Turkey and North Africa —people live without the comforts we take for granted as part of everyday life.

The system of property ownership goes a long way towards explaining the lack of modern agricultural techniques and the tremendous gap between rich and poor. Often wealthy absentee landlords own large estates worked by farm laborers who are paid very low wages. In Sicily and southern Italy, agricultural workers live in towns and travel out every day to the fields. Elsewhere, farmers who own or rent their own small acreages of often infertile land, barely grow enough to feed their own families. They grow a little grain, corn, keep a few sheep, goats and chickens, perhaps have some olive trees and a small vegetable garden. Many people in rural areas live in rude houses made of mud bricks or boulders from the mountains, with only the simplest necessities for comfortable living.

There are more than enough people to work the relatively small farmland areas. Industrial jobs are few and far between. So it is not surprising that many people, especially Italians, have emigrated to the United States, and the better job opportunities in Northwest Europe.

In Yugoslavia agrarian reform has helped narrow the gap between rich and poor. The government has broken up big estates and re-allocated land to peasants. Italy is also working on a similar program. Egypt, Spain and North African countries are also taking the first steps towards dealing with this enormous problem. Israel has perhaps found the best solution with *kibbutzim*, land units that are worked communally.

Another reason for low living standards in the Mediterranean is that everything moves slowly. Agriculture never moves as fast as industry; but in the Mediterranean the hot weather makes people lethargic. In summer, even in the cities, life stops for two or three hours after lunch for the *siesta*. Later, things liven up, shops reopen and everyone —except the many unemployed—resumes work.

Population density in this area is an average of about 150 people per square mile. Most of the urban population live in the great capital cities—Athens, Rome, Madrid, Lisbon, Algiers, Tunis, and Cairo; industrial centers like Turin, Milan and Bologne; or industrial ports: Genoa, Naples, Venice, Trieste, Salonika, Barcelona and Casablanca. In the country people crowd together in well-watered areas like the Po Valley, and the small plains of southern Italy, Egypt and Spain. But large open spaces like the Spanish Meseta, the Greek mountains and especially the Libyan desert are almost empty.

Left: The Grand Harbor at Valletta, the capital of Malta. An independent country of the British Commonwealth since 1962, Malta's elaborate fortifications, including Senglea Point (center background), were chiefly the work of the Knights of St. John who held the island 1530–1798.

Below: a fish market scene at Chioggia, at the southern end of the Venetian lagoon. The port is linked with the mainland by a bridge. Chioggia, while mainly a fishing port, is also engaged in shipbuilding and the coastal trade.

Most people around the Mediterranean belong to one racial, or *ethnic*, group. They are short and dark-haired with olive or brown skins. But on the coasts of southern Europe you find signs of the Alpine influence. People are still short and stocky, but they have lighter skins and hair. In the eastern Mediterranean and along the North African coast the Arabian influence becomes predominant, marked by greater height and slighter build. Yugoslavia touches on slavic Eastern Europe. In western Europe some small groups, like the isolated Basques in the western end of the Pyrenees, have kept their own separate characteristics and languages intact.

Great empires of the past have left marks on all the languages spoken in the Mediterranean region. Modern Greek is confined within the borders of the country, but Latin influences have spread through all the languages of southern Europe—Italian, Portugese, Spanish. Arabic is spoken in the vast region that takes up North Africa and the Eastern Mediterranean. In Israel Hebrew has become a living language again. For centuries Jews left their homeland in Palestine and set up communities all over Europe. But since the formation of the state of Israel in 1948, many of their descendants have returned, bringing modern skills and techniques.

Two great religions, Christianity and Islam, dominate the Mediterranean. Christianity, born in Palestine, spread all through Europe. There are two separate Christian churches: The Greek Orthodox, centered in Istanbul, has most of its adherents in Greece and neighboring countries of Eastern Europe. The Roman Catholic Church is under the authority of the Pope, ruler of the 109-acre independent Vatican State. Most Italians, Frenchmen, Portugese and Spaniards are Roman Catholics.

More than 1,000 years ago, Arabs took Islam right across North Africa and even into southern Spain. They built mosques with minarets and onion-shaped domes. Some Spanish architecture still reflects Arab influence. Turkey is also a Moslem country and there are small groups of Mohammedans in Greece, Bulgaria and Yugoslavia.

The Mediterranean and the World

The Mediterranean has a unique place in the story of mankind. It was the cradle of Western civilization. The seeds of that civilization were sown about 5,000 years ago in Crete, the island home of cultured seafarers, and then took root in mainland Greece. Greek traders and colonists in turn spread knowledge of science, art and philosophy throughout the Mediterranean.

Other places and peoples added their contributions. Rome's vast empire contributed the Roman system of law, which forms the basis of much of the present day legal systems in the West. Palestine, in the Levant, was the birthplace of Christianity. From Italy, in much later times, came the glories of Renaissance philosophy and culture. Two great seafaring nations of the region, Spain and Portugal, sent out explorers to find new trade routes to the East and new lands across the oceans. Their success led to a decline in the importance of the Mediterranean. Its lands and waters were no longer the main highway for the spices, silks and other Eastern luxuries. Northwest Europe was beginning to exploit its natural advantages, and for a time it seemed that the Mediterranean would become a backwater, no longer a world center of ideas and power.

The situation was radically changed by the opening of the Suez Canal in 1869. This new shortened sea route to the East was vitally important to Britain, whose empire embraced India and territories in Africa and the Far East; and it gave added significance to British Mediterranean bases like Gibraltar and Malta. Britain's hold on the Suez Canal itself ended in 1956 when the United Arab Republic (Egypt) seized control.

In the Mediterranean, as in other regions, there have been many political changes since World War II. In the east the state of Israel has been created from part of Palestine, and Cyprus has become independent. Malta, marking the division of the Mediterranean into its western and eastern basins, is also independent. The former French territories on the African shore—Morocco, Algeria and Tunisia—have won independence too. Their economic links with Europe, however, remain strong. The Mediterranean is still strategically important to both the United States and the U.S.S.R., since it is one of the major water routes between the two powers and gives access to the Black Sea, where the U.S.S.R. has its only ice-free winter ports.

Top: folk dancers in Corfu wear colorful national costume. Corfu, one of the Ionian Islands, stands at the entrance to the Adriatic Sea, separated from Greece and Albania by the Corfu Channel. Its chief town, also called Corfu, is on the east coast.

Opposite page: the acropolis ("high city") was the fortress heart of most city states in ancient Greece. The Acropolis of Athens still dominates the Greek capital. This dramatic night view shows the Parthenon—a temple dedicated to the goddess Athena and a lasting symbol of the glory that was Greece.

COUNTRIES OF THE MEDITERRANEAN

ALBANIA*
Republic
S. Europe
Area: 11,000 sq. miles

Pop: 1,914,000. **Land use %:** wasteland 24; forest and mountain pasture 34; meadow land and pasture 30; cultivated 12. **Occupations:** agriculture, stock raising (goats, sheep, cattle). **Industries:** connected mainly with agriculture, e.g. flour milling, cheese making. A little mining (chrome, copper, salt), olive oil, cotton and woollen fabric manufacture. **Capital:** Tirana (153,000).

ALGERIA*
Republic
N. Africa
Area: 919,000 sq. miles

Pop: 12,000,000. **Land use %:** cultivated 3; permanent meadow and pastureland 19; forest and woodland 1; wasteland 77. **Occupations:** agriculture (grain, vines, fruit), pastoral (sheep, goats, cattle, camels), mining (iron and phosphates). **Industries:** petroleum, manufacturing on a small scale. **Capital:** Algiers (943,000).

CYPRUS* †
Republic
E. Mediterranean
Area: 4,000 sq. miles

Pop: 603,000. **Land use %:** arable 47; waste 25; forest and woodland 18; meadow and pasture 10. **Occupations:** agriculture, manufacturing, mining. **Industries:** textiles, clothing, food processing, light metal goods. **Capital:** Nicosia (106,000).

GREECE*
Kingdom
S.E. Europe
Area: 51,000 sq. miles

Pop: 8,612,000. **Land use %:** meadow and pasture 39; arable 26; waste 20; forest and woodland 15. **Occupations:** agriculture, manufacturing. **Industries:** textiles, chemicals, cement, glass. **Capital:** Athens (1,853,000).

ISRAEL*
Republic
S.W. Asia
Area: 8,000 sq. miles

Pop: 2,643,000. **Land use %:** waste, pasture, etc. 84; cultivated 16. **Occupations:** industry, trade, agriculture. **Industries:** food processing, chemicals, textiles, light engineering. **Capital:** Jerusalem (192,000).

ITALY*
Republic
S. Europe
Area: 116,000 sq. miles

Pop: 53,000,000. **Land use %:** arable 55; forest and woodland 20; meadow and pasture 17; waste 8. **Occupations:** agriculture, industry, commerce. **Industries:** textiles, iron and steel products, shipbuilding, automobiles, clothing, chemicals, handicrafts. **Capital:** Rome (2,514,000).

JORDAN*
Kingdom
S.W. Asia
Area: 30,000 sq. miles

Pop: 2,017,000. **Land use %:** waste 88; pasture 7; cultivated 5; grassland 2. **Occupations:** agriculture, pastoral. **Industries:** phosphates, minor crafts. **Capital:** Amman (342,000).

LEBANON*
Republic
S.W. Asia
Area: 4,300 sq. miles

Pop: 2,405,000. **Land use %:** waste 65; cultivated 27; forest and woodland 7; meadow and pasture 1. **Occupations:** mainly agriculture, manufacturing trade. **Industry:** textiles, oil refining, leather. **Capital:** Beirut (500,000).

LIBYA*
Kingdom
N. Africa
Area: 679,000 sq. miles

Pop: 1,677,000. **Land use %:** waste 92; grassland 6; cultivated 2. **Occupations:** petroleum, farming. **Industries:** handicrafts and textiles, leather and metal goods. **Capital:** Tripoli (232,000) and Benghazi (108,000). **Capital designate:** Beida.

MALTA, G.C.* †
Constitutional Monarchy
Central Mediterranean Sea
Area: 122 sq. miles

Pop: 318,000. **Land use %:** cultivated 53; waste 47. **Occupations:** agriculture, fishing, trading. **Industries:** dockyards, consumer goods, tourism. **Capital:** Valletta (18,000).

MONACO
Principality
N. Mediterranean
Area: 368 acres

Pop: 22,000. **Land use:** all urban (built up). **Occupations:** commerce, tourism. **Capital:** Monaco (2,400).

1 ALBANIA
2 ALGERIA
3 CYPRUS
4 GREECE
5 ISRAEL
6 ITALY
7 JORDAN
8 LEBANON
9 LIBYA
10 MALTA, G. C.
11 MONACO
12 MOROCCO
13 PORTUGAL
14 SAN MARINO
15 SPAIN
16 SYRIA
17 TUNISIA
18 TURKEY
19 UNITED ARAB REPUBLIC (EGYPT)
20 VATICAN CITY
21 YUGOSLAVIA

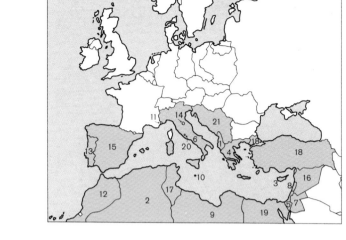

MOROCCO*
Kingdom
N.W. Africa
Area: 173,000 sq. miles

Pop: 13,451,000. **Land use %:** waste 51; cultivated 21; grassland 19; forest 9. **Occupations:** agriculture, mining, fishing. **Industries:** processing agricultural and mineral products, handicrafts. **Capital:** Rabat (261,000).

PORTUGAL*
Republic
S.W. Europe
Area: 35,000 sq. miles

Pop: 9,218,000. **Land use %:** cultivated and pastureland 38; waste 34; forest and woodland 28. **Occupations:** agriculture, manufacturing. **Industries:** mining, lumbering, textiles, pottery, chemicals. **Capital:** Lisbon (820,000). **Overseas Provinces:** Cape Verde Islands, Guinea, S. Tomé and Principé, Angola, Mozambique, Macao, Timor.

SAN MARINO
Republic
Northern Apennines of Italy
Area: 24 sq. miles

Pop: 17,000. **Land use:** mainly agriculture. **Industries:** food processing, stone masonry. **Capital:** San Marino (2,000).

SPAIN*
Nominal Monarchy
S.W. Europe
Area: 195,000 sq. miles

Pop: 31,871,000. **Land use %:** meadow and pasture 47; cultivated 38; forest and woodland 10; waste 5. **Occupations:** agriculture, forestry, fishing, manufacturing. **Industries:** iron and steel, textiles, mining, leather goods, ceramics, light engineering. **Capital:** Madrid (2,559,000). **Provinces in Africa:** Spanish Guinea—Rio Muni and Fernando Po; Spanish West Africa—Ifni and Spanish Sahara.

SYRIA*
Republic
E. Mediterranean
Area: 72,000 sq. miles

Pop: 5,634,000. **Land use %:** waste 48; meadow and pasture 31; cultivated 19; forest 2. **Occupations:** agriculture. **Industries:** textiles, processing of agricultural products. **Capital:** Damascus (599,000).

TUNISIA*
Republic
N. Africa
Area: 48,000 sq. miles

Pop: 4,458,000. **Land use %:** waste 42; grassland 28; cultivated 24; forest 6. **Occupations:** agriculture, fishing, mining. **Industries:** processing dates, olives, cereals. **Capital:** Tunis (764,000).

TURKEY*
Republic
S.E. Europe and S.W. Asia
Area: 301,000 sq. miles

Pop: 32,901,000. **Land use %:** meadow and pasture 50; cultivated 20; waste 17; forest and woodland 13. **Occupations:** agriculture, mining, manufacturing. **Industries:** iron and steel, textiles, paper, food stuffs, fertilizers, glass, soap. **Capital:** Ankara (902,000).

UNITED ARAB REPUBLIC (EGYPT)*
Republic
N.E. Africa
Area: 386,000 sq. miles

Pop: 30,147,000. **Land use %:** waste 98; cultivated 2. **Occupations:** agriculture, manufacturing, commerce. **Industries:** consumer goods, textiles, foodstuffs, tobacco. **Capital:** Cairo (4,000,000).

VATICAN CITY
Papal State
Rome, Italy
Area: 109 acres

Pop: 1,000. **Capital:** Vatican City.

YUGOSLAVIA*
Republic
S. Europe
Area: 99,000 sq. miles

Pop: 19,756,000. **Land use %:** forest and woodland 34; cultivated 30; meadow and pasture 23; waste 13. **Occupations:** agriculture, industry, mining. **Industries:** metal working, textiles, foodstuffs and other consumer goods. **Capital:** Belgrade (963,000).

* Member of the United Nations
† Member of the British Commonwealth

3

ARABIA AND AFRICA

Africa has an area of 11 million square miles and is the second largest continent. Its desert belt, including the vast Sahara, stretches across the north and into Arabia, which is also linked historically and racially with North Africa. During the 19th century "scramble for Africa" European nations took over almost the whole continent, but most former colonies are now independent.

Street scene in the older part of Cairo suggests that little has changed over the years. The city, which is the capital of the United Arab Republic (Egypt), stands mainly on the right bank of the Nile. It is the largest city in Africa and continues to make rapid growth. For a contrast between the old Cairo (left) and the new, see page 51.

Tropical Desert

Stretching across North Africa, and continuing into and beyond the peninsula of Arabia, is the world's hottest, driest desert. Few people live here since it is wild, desolate country with sand, bare rock and little or no vegetation. There are many sand dunes, constantly shifted by the wind, and a lot of bare rock and pebbles. The rock is swept clean of sand and often stands out in unusual shapes molded by wind erosion. The desert is usually arid, but in the central Sahara there are dry channels or *wadis* where water sometimes flows after torrential rain. The Sahara and Arabia both show traces of a time, comparatively recent, when a more humid climate prevailed and there were true rivers.

Desert plants are specially adapted to withstand prolonged dryness. Some have long roots or fleshy, thick-stemmed leaves and stems to keep in moisture. Some plants store water in their stems. Seeds may lie dormant for a long time just beneath the surface and only grow and flower after rain. Animal life is as scarce as plant life. Aside from domestic animals kept by nomadic tribes, only antelopes and desert foxes roam the sands.

The reason this region is so dry is that the winds usually blow from the center of the Asian continent and carry little moisture. Only about ten inches of rain falls a year, usually in violent showers. After a downpour it quickly disappears. Sometimes, for several years in succession, there is no rain at all.

The heat is scorching. Temperatures in summer may reach well over 100°F. and noon temperatures often reach 120°F. in the shade. The surface of the earth heats up very quickly and may reach 170°F. —so hot that if you broke an egg on a sidewalk in North Africa it would fry in a few seconds. Winter temperatures average 60°–70°F.

Clear, cloudless skies make the days very hot. But in the desert the earth cools very quickly after sundown and the nights are very cold. There is

Moving an oil rig to a new site south of Tobruk, Libya. Just how much oil there is in this federal kingdom still has to be discovered. Currently, more than 30 oil companies are prospecting. Meanwhile, increasing quantities are being piped to the coast from Zelten, Dahra and other fields.

often a frost at dawn because the air is cold and dry. Night skies are clear with a bright moon and sparkling stars.

Some people live in desert regions because they have to, others because they always have. The first category includes engineers, technicians and government administrators; and the second, nomadic tribes who wander with their camels, sheep and goats, accustomed to a hard life and poor pastures. The oasis dwellers are more fortunate.

There is water in some places even in a desert. The Tibesti Mountains in northern Chad and the Ahaggar Mountains in Algeria have springs and streams. In Libya the water lies in porous layers of rock near the surface, so people can get to it by digging wells. In some places the water comes naturally to the surface, forming small pools around which date palms cluster. These places are called *oases;* some are small, others are many miles across and have houses and small fields around the pools and wells.

There are two great oases in this desert region;

the land bordering the Nile, and the valley of the Tigris and Euphrates Rivers in Iraq. It was in the Tigris/Euphrates valley that men, using the river water for irrigation, established one of the earliest civilizations. The area between the two rivers is known for its beautiful palm groves and produces dates of the highest quality.

The Nile valley was also the center of an early civilization. Herodotus wrote that Egypt was "the gift of the Nile". The Upper Nile has two main tributaries, the White Nile and the Blue Nile. Lake Victoria, which is almost as big as Maine, is the source of the White Nile. From this great lake on the Equator, the White Nile flows down through the Sudan and spreads out through large swamps, called the Sudd. A lot of water is lost by evaporation in these swamps and engineers are trying to clear the channels to increase the river's flow. The Blue Nile begins at Lake Tana in the Abyssinian Highlands and joins the White Nile at Khartoum, bringing great floods of water in summer.

Since early times the people of the Nile valley

Top: the turbine house of the Aswan High Dam, under construction on the Nile River in Egypt, will supply Cairo with electricity.

have tried to control its waters. Today the major dam installations are at Aswan, Asyut and Sennar. Below Aswan a green ribbon of fertile land stretches along the banks of the Nile. It is only 10 miles wide; beyond lie the sand and rock of the desert. Crops can be grown all year in this carefully irrigated strip, and it is densely populated, with more than 500 people to the square mile. The new Aswan High Dam, completed in 1965, has increased water storage capacity and will dramatically increase the area under irrigation. Cairo (population four million) stands in the Nile valley; it is the largest city in the whole of Africa.

Map of the Nile Valley. The Nile, Africa's greatest river, rises in Lake Victoria and flows more than 4,000 miles down to its great delta on the Mediterranean. Its valley from Aswan to the delta is a green ribbon of fertile land never more than 10 miles wide, with barren, dry desert on either side. The lower Nile valley was a cradle of early civilization. As long ago as 5000 B.C. farmers used the river to irrigate crops. (Scale: 295 miles to the inch).

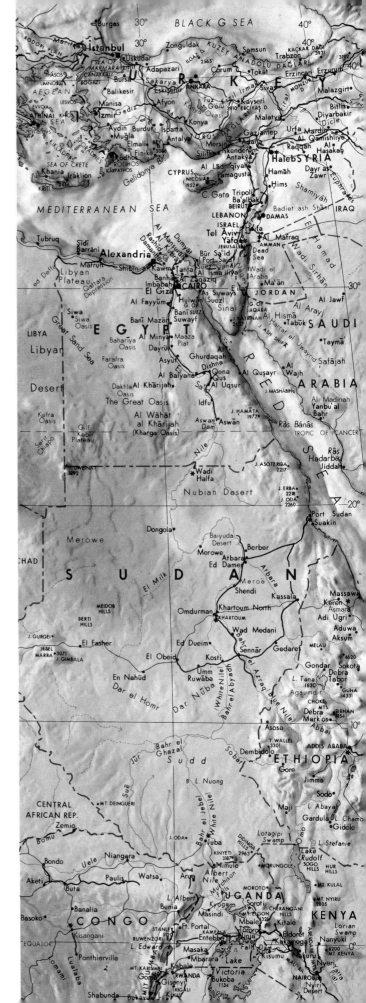

Tropical Forests and Grasslands

Right: the Congo, one of the world's great rivers, is about 3,000 miles long. Its course through the hot steaming forests of central equatorial Africa is sometimes interrupted by falls and rapids. In some areas the vegetation is so dense that the river is the only highway.

Broadly, Africa has east-west bands of climate and vegetation running parallel with the Equator. The Sahara Desert extends across the extreme north; dry tropical grasslands lie south of it; then comes wet equatorial forest. South of the Equator there is grassland again, and then desert.

Occasional baobab trees with enormous trunks and bare branches punctuate the *savanna* grassland south of the Sahara. Near the desert, the grass is short and tufty, but farther south where there is more rain, the grass may be 12 feet high. Trees grow in clumps or along river banks. This "brush country" is the natural home of big game like elephants, lions, giraffes and gazelles.

On the eastern side of the continent the east-west pattern is interrupted by high ground. The savanna grassland, scattered with trees and bushes, continues south across the Equator and onto the East African Plateau, between 3,000 and 6,000 feet high. Because of its altitude the plateau has a cool, invigorating climate and a dry season.

The East African Plateau includes Kenya, Uganda, Tanzania, Rhodesia, Zambia, Malawi and Ethiopia. In the north rise the rugged massive mountains of the Abyssinian Highlands. South of the Equator, the highest peak in Africa, Mount Kilimanjaro (19,340 feet) wears a permanent snow cap. Mount Kenya, almost on the Equator, is 17,058 feet high and has several glaciers.

The whole plateau is scored by a huge system of rift valleys. Lakes Malawi and Rudolf, the Red Sea, the Gulf of Aqaba and the Dead Sea lie in one huge valley stretching from East Africa through to Jordan. This deep, steep-sided valley is from 20 to 50 miles wide. To the west Lake Tanganyika, Lake Kivu, Lake Edward and Lake Albert lie in another line of rift valleys. And between these two systems is broad, shallow Lake Victoria, the largest of the African lakes and the third largest lake in the world.

West of the East African Plateau and south of the savanna grassland, the trees become more numerous with the increase in rainfall and the decrease in altitude. Dense equatorial forests run along the west

coast of Africa from Guinea to the Congo and cover half the Congo basin. Rainfall is heavy all year (60–100 inches) and there is no dry season; temperatures average 75°F. all year. In this warm humid climate the trees often grow to 100 feet high and under their dense foliage all kinds of forest plants struggle up to reach the light. Birds, some with bright plumage, fly above the treetops, monkeys swing and leap from branch to branch, snakes move silently through the forest gloom. To travel through the dense undergrowth is not easy; travelers must cut their way through. The only real routes are the large rivers, teeming with fish and crocodiles.

Southern Africa has a variety of territories—the Republic of South Africa, South-West Africa, the Portuguese provinces of Angola and Mozambique, and Botswana, Lesotho and Swaziland.

Below the Congo basin the climate becomes drier and there is grassland. The western side of the continent is mostly desert—the Namib Desert along the coast and the Kalahari Desert inland. Between the deserts and the well-forested Drakensberg Mountains, rising to 11,000 feet in the east like a great wall overlooking the Indian Ocean, is the grassland plateau which South Africans call the Veld. Between 1834 and 1838 the Boers (Dutch farmers in South Africa) came to the Veld to escape British rule—a migration known in South African history as "the Great Trek".

Southern Africa is cooler than the rest of the continent because it is farther from the Equator and because much of it has an altitude of more than 6,000 feet. The Cape Town area has a Mediterranean climate. Temperatures average 50°F. during the warm, moist winters; summers are hot and dry, with average temperatures of 70°F. The impact of the European way of life has been stronger in Southern Africa than in any other part of the continent, except perhaps Algeria.

Above: Kru surf boats at Accra, the capital of Ghana. Here the Atlantic surf is so heavy that ships used to lie offshore and load or unload cargo by surf boat. The new harbor at Tema, 17 miles east of Accra, opened in 1962, now handles most of this trade. Below: Cape Town is the legislative capital and second largest city of the republic of South Africa. It has a fine harbor sheltered by the surrounding mountains. A famous landmark is flat-topped Table Mountain (3,549 feet) immediately behind the city.

Except for palm oil, peanuts and certain hardwoods, the chief commercial crops of Africa have mostly been introduced from abroad. They include cotton, cacao, rubber, tobacco, sugar, the grape vine, corn, coffee and tea. Many of the everyday food crops of tropical Africa—yams, sweet potatoes, corn and bananas—were also introduced by Europeans.

Fine-quality cotton is a leading export crop in the U.A.R. (Egypt) and the Sudan; Uganda's cotton exports are also important. Other producers include Cameroun, the Central African Republic, Nigeria, Mali and Chad, but neither Nigeria nor Mali exports cotton. At Fort Archambault (Chad), a cotton textile industry is being developed.

More than half the world's supply of cocoa comes from Ghana and Western Nigeria, where the cacao tree is cultivated on a large scale. Nigeria, like Gambia and Senegal, grows large crops of peanuts. The oil palm, grown mainly in coastal areas of the Gulf of Guinea, yields great clusters of plum-like fruits. A lot of the oil produced by crushing these is exported for soap and margarine manufacture. There are large rubber plantations in Liberia; rubber is also an export crop of the Congo.

Coffee needs good soil, warmth and moisture, and shade from strong sun. It is grown by farmers on the East African Plateau (Kenya and Uganda) and in Ethiopia, where it also grows wild, it is the most important cash crop.

Tobacco is Rhodesia's most important commercial crop. Sisal, a drought-resisting plant whose fiber is used in making binder twine, grows well in some parts of Kenya, Uganda and Tanzania. The island of Zanzibar, since 1964 a part of Tanzania, provides most of the world's cloves. Tea is grown in Malawi, Tanzania, Uganda, Kenya, Rhodesia and the Congo. Sugar is of major importance in Natal, and is also grown in Kenya, Malawi, Mozambique, Rhodesia, Somalia, Egypt and Uganda.

But many Africans are still subsistence farmers. The savanna grasslands are too dry for commercial crops, but millet is grown as a food crop. Farmers also keep cattle, but they are usually riddled with disease caused by the tsetse fly. This same fly causes a human disease, sleeping sickness, the scourge of tropical Africa.

West of the Drakensberg Mountains the climate is warm and moist enough for corn growing. Cattle and sheep thrive, free from the tsetse fly. In Cape Province, at the extreme southern tip of Africa, the climate is like Algeria's and is ideal for winter wheat, vines, citrus fruits, peaches and apricots.

Africans fish everywhere along the coasts, and in the lakes and rivers. Mackerel, mullet, snoek and sole are the chief sea varieties caught. In Zambia fish farming is being developed. Uganda's lakes and rivers make up one of the largest freshwater fisheries in the world.

Africa is rich in mineral resources. Some metals have been mined and worked for centuries. The antique iron work and bronzes of Benin (Nigeria) are among the finest examples of African art. But exploitation of minerals in the modern sense has only developed within the last hundred years.

Hassi Messaoud, one of the chief oil fields in the Algerian Sahara, is linked by a 400-mile pipeline with the port of Bougie. Other important Algerian fields include Edjélé, which has a pipeline to Skirra (Tunisia) and El Gassi. Natural gas has been found at Djebel Berga and Hassi-R'Mel.

The modern part of Cairo contrasts sharply with the old (page 44). Its new office blocks, fashionable hotels, smart shops and restaurants, and busy, well-lit streets are not unlike those in the great cities of western countries. The climate is mild in winter, but very hot and dry in summer.

The discovery of diamonds along and east of the Vaal River, South Africa, led to the founding of Kimberley in 1871. Today the city has some of the world's largest diamond mines and produces mostly gem stones. Coastal stretches of South-West Africa are an important source of industrial diamonds, and these are also mined in Sierra Leone. Another South African city, Johannesburg, was founded by goldminers in 1886 and is now the commercial center of the Rand, the world's greatest gold-mining area. Gold is also mined in several other African countries.

The Katanga province of the Congo is another great mineral producer. Here, and across the border in Zambia, are rich but fairly shallow copper mines —the source of one fifth of the world's copper. Uranium, too, is mined in this area. Ghana and Guinea have bauxite, the mineral from which aluminium is made. Liberia has numerous lead mines; Sierra Leone, the world's largest proven reserves of rutile, used in making paint pigments and titanium metals.

Generally Africa is not rich in coal. The Wankie coal field in Rhodesia, the coal fields in Natal and near Johannesburg, South Africa, meet only local needs. The huge deposits of iron ore around Fort Gouraud, Mauritania, are now being worked and exported by a new railway to Port Étienne on the coast. Algeria, the republic of South Africa and other countries have iron ore, too.

Petroleum and natural gas are being exploited in the Algerian Sahara and in Libya. The countries around the Persian Gulf are a major source of oil for western Europe. Hydroelectric development includes the Kariba Dam on the Zambezi, the Owen Falls Dam in Uganda, and the Volta River Dam in Ghana.

Cocoa farming in Ghana. The crop is harvested October–December, but there is a second harvest about April. The beans are matured in heaps covered with leaves, then dried and bagged. The entire crop is sold through a Government marketing board.

51

Life in Arabia and Africa

Wood carving of West African drummers. Once used extensively to send messages from village to village, drums still play an important part in African folk dance and ceremony.

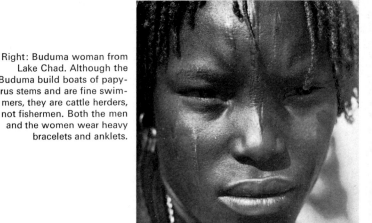

Right: Buduma woman from Lake Chad. Although the Buduma build boats of papyrus stems and are fine swimmers, they are cattle herders, not fishermen. Both the men and the women wear heavy bracelets and anklets.

The great peninsula of Arabia has an area of about 1,200,000 square miles, but a population of only 20 million. This is because most of Arabia is inhospitable desert, where nomads move from waterhole to waterhole with their camels. Most people, however, live in the oases, especially in the north and east of the Nejd (Saudi Arabia), the chief breeding ground of the famous Arab horses. Fertile areas on the fringes of Arabia include the Yemen, where Mocha coffee is grown. Iraq, the land of the Tigris and Euphrates rivers, is rich in oil and is also the world's chief producer of dates. These grow around Basra, the chief port.

The discovery of oil has transformed Arabia. Apart from Iraq, with its Mosul and Kirkuk oil fields, there are the oil states of the Persian Gulf.

Small sheikdoms like Bahrein, Kuwait and Qatar have become rich and important. Saudi Arabia is one of the leading oil producers in the Middle East. Although the wealth flowing in as the oil flows out has often remained in the hands of a few, an increasing amount of money is being devoted to social services and industrial development.

Africa is still an essentially agricultural continent. Most Africans still make their living from the land, using primitive methods of cultivation; or hunt and fish. Many African governments, however, now have social and economic development programs and conditions are gradually improving.

One early change was the introduction of cash crops and plantations. Early industries were directly related to readily available raw materials—for example, the palm oil processing plants of Nigeria and Egyptian cotton mills. Now the emerging African states are trying to develop their mineral resources. They want more industrialization, but have been held up by the lack of capital and technical knowledge, except when they have been able to get monetary and technical aid from abroad. South Africa is still the only country with a highly developed industrial complex.

Lack of good communications also hampers economic growth. Transportation is a major problem in this continent, where most roads are made of earth and gravel and are often impassable in the rainy season. Rivers are only partly navigable because of the many waterfalls and rapids, and there are relatively few natural harbors. South Africa is the only country with an extensive railroad system. But African governments are working, with assistance from outside, to improve their communications systems. A new railroad between Tanzania and Zambia is to be planned with Chinese and Anglo-Canadian help; China has promised to

finance its construction. West Germany is building a new port for Togo at Lomé. But these are only the beginnings of a solution to an immense problem.

The 303 million people of Africa are distributed unevenly over the continent. The Nile valley and delta, the East African Plateau, the Guinea coast and the coast of southeast Africa are well populated. But hardly anyone lives in the deserts of North Africa and the Kalahari.

Considering the size of the continent, Africa has few large cities. Only four—Cairo, Kinshasa, Alexandria and Johannesburg—have populations of more than one million. Other cities, like Algiers, Tunis, Lagos, Ibadan, Addis Ababa, Pretoria, Durban, Cape Town, Ogbomoshu and Salisbury are growing fast. Africans are drifting into the towns; rapid urban growth often leads to ugly groups of slum shacks on the outskirts of towns and cities.

Light-skinned people—Berbers, Arabs and Egyptians—live in North Africa and Arabia. But south of the Sahara the Negroid type predominates. It includes the tall, ebony black Sudanese of the forest and savanna; Nilotic tribes like the Dinka and Nuer; and Bantu tribes like the Swahili, Zulu, Basuto and Kaffirs. There are Guinean tribes like the Ashanti of Ghana and the Yoruba of Nigeria. There are the Congolese or "Forest Negro" people; they are easily recognized by the unusual raised scars they produce on their skins—a practice known as cicatrisation. Most Congo tribes are shorter than the Guineans; and the shortest of all are the pygmies. Southwest Africa has the lighter skinned Bushmen, Hottentots and Hereros. Another group includes the Ethiopians, Somalis and Masai. In South Africa there are about $3\frac{1}{4}$ million Europeans, speaking Afrikaans and English, and small groups of Indians and Chinese.

Top: new buildings in Addis Ababa, the capital of Ethiopia, house the Commercial Bank (round building) and the National Bank (tall building). Because Addis Ababa stands about 8,000 feet above sea level its climate is healthy.

Below: Mecca, the birthplace of Mohammed, the founder of Islam. All Moslems hope to make a pilgrimage to the city at least once in their lives and to kiss the sacred Black Stone built into the east corner of the silk-covered Kaaba (cube).

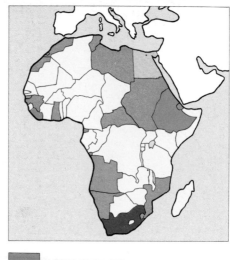

Independent before 1900

1900-1919

1920-1939

1940-1959

1960-1967

Still awaiting independence

The map shows how European colonization has disappeared almost entirely from Africa. Progress to independence was especially rapid after World War II and there are now only a handful of territories under colonial rule.

Africa is a continent of great contrasts. Its landscape ranges from the steaming forests of the Congo to the burning deserts of the Sahara and Kalahari; its people, from the tall, light-skinned Berbers of North Africa to the short, dark-skinned people of the Congo. There are hundreds of different languages and dialects, customs, traditions and ways of life.

The continent has felt the influence of settlers from many different European countries, each group bringing its own ideas and ways of life. Probably the extreme diversity of colonizing nations helps explain why Africa, unlike North America and western Europe, has no single unifying culture.

Africa has changed rapidly in the last half century. Before World War I there were only three independent states—Ethiopia, Liberia and the Union (now Republic) of South Africa. Ethiopia, Christian empire since the fourth century A.D., is the only state with a long history of self-government. Legend dates it from the meeting of King Solomon and the Queen of Sheba. Liberia was founded in 1822 by freed Negro slaves with the help of American colonization societies. Monrovia, its capital, was named after President James Monroe. The name Liberia comes from the Latin word *liber* meaning "free". South Africa became a dominion of the British Commonwealth of Nations in 1910, but left the Commonwealth in 1961 and became a republic.

Most of Africa is now independent, except Mozambique, Angola and other Portuguese territories, and small Spanish territories on the west coast. Most countries became independent quite peacefully.

But in equatorial Africa there was widespread violence in the Belgian colony of the Congo when it gained independence in 1960 and the United Nations had to intervene. Even this did not pacify the country entirely and it remained at the mercy of ambitious politicians, rival armies and foreign mercenaries. Algeria, too, was the scene of bitter fighting before it won independence from the French in 1962.

The Federation of Rhodesia and Nyasaland was

a shortlived British attempt to make one nation out of the two Rhodesias and Nyasaland. This project did not win the support of the African peoples involved. So Northern Rhodesia and Nyasaland went their own ways as the independent Commonwealth republics of Zambia and Malawi. The future of the third member of the old federation, Rhodesia, still has to be determined. In 1965 the Rhodesian Government issued a unilateral declaration of independence, but its validity was not recognized by the British Government.

It is not surprising that although the African countries have achieved independence, their political institutions and economic organization have a European flavor. For example, if you move west from Ghana into the neighboring Ivory Coast, you know immediately that you have left a former British territory and entered what was formerly a French colony. Now the influence of other countries, including the Soviet Union, China, India and Japan, is gaining ground. The newly independent African countries are more concerned with fast economic development than with east-west political alignments.

There are so many problems. Africans want more education (most can neither read nor write), more technical progress and more industry. At the same

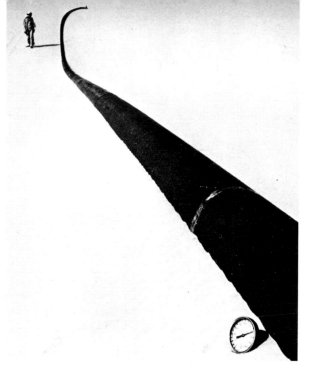

Pipeline connects Abqaiq, the chief oil field of Saudi Arabia, with the large refinery at Ras Tanura. But a lot of crude oil is piped west along the 1068-mile long TAPline (Trans-Arabian Pipeline) to the Mediterranean port of Saida. Saudi Arabia is a leading world oil producer.

time they are grappling with the transformation of tribal rule and colonial aftermath into government of a nation. Tribal differences and disagreements have to be smoothed out and a sense of national unity created. Even everyday administration is a problem since many more trained officials are needed than are usually available.

Africa's most complex problem is in South Africa, a country settled by white and black people coming from different directions at the same time. Political power is in the hands of the whites, and the official policy is *Apartheid*—Afrikaans for apartness or separation. Broadly this means that whites and non-whites live in different areas of the country and develop separately. About 13 per cent of the country has been earmarked as tribal reserves or *bantustans* in which most of the Bantu people—about two thirds of the total population of over 18 million—will be required to live.

In practice white and non-white groups overlap. The non-whites, including "coloreds" and Indians, have only limited political rights in their non-white areas. But non-whites living in white areas have no political rights at all. This arbitrary racial division causes intense dissatisfaction not only among non-white South Africans, but also in the newly independent countries of Africa.

Top: stamps of Zambia (President Kaunda with a background of Victoria Falls); Malawi (Head of President Banda); Tanzania (Sultan of Zanzibar and view of the Mangapwani Cave); and Lesotho (Moshoeshoe I, first paramount chief, and Moshoeshoe II, first king of independent Lesotho).

Library of University College, Ibadan, Nigeria. Nigeria urgently needs more trained teachers and more schools. Ibadan, Nigeria's largest city, is an important trading center (cocoa, cotton and palm oil) and the administrative capital of Western Nigeria.

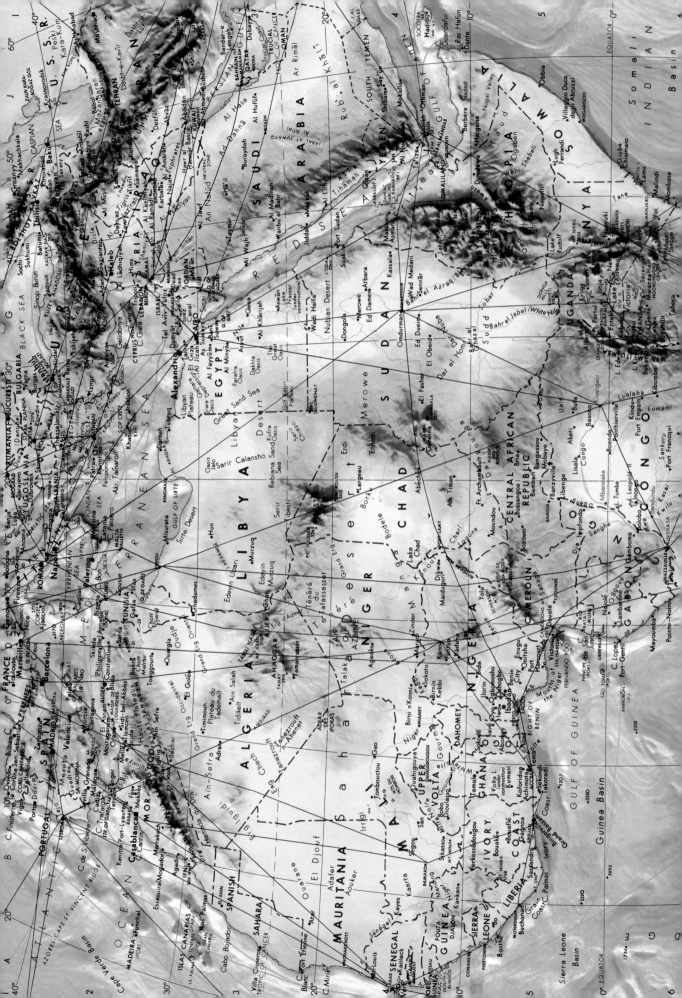

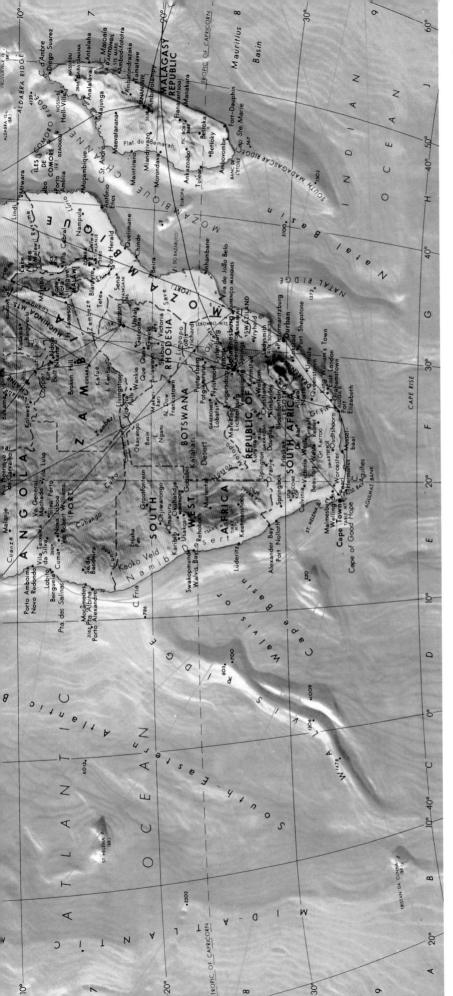

Africa

Projection: Lambert's Equal Area
Heights and depths in metres

Scale: 1:27,300,000

Miles
0   200   400   600

0   200   400   600   800   1000   1200
Kilometres

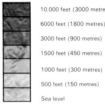
10,000 feet (3000 metres)
6000 feet (1800 metres)
3000 feet (900 metres)
1500 feet (450 metres)
1000 feet (300 metres)
500 feet (150 metres)
Sea level

Towns:
■ over 1,000,000
● over 500,000
• over 250,000
· under 250,000

⌒ International boundaries
⌒ Boundaries under dispute
⌒ Major air routes
⌒ Major sea routes

COUNTRIES OF ARABIA AND AFRICA

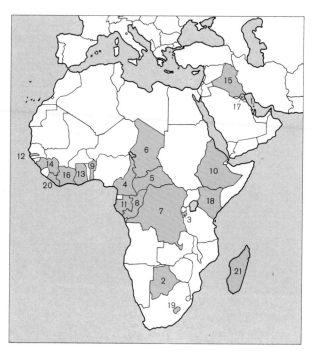

1 BAHREIN
2 BOTSWANA
3 BURUNDI
4 CAMEROUN
5 CENTRAL AFRICAN REPUBLIC
6 CHAD
7 CONGO
8 REPUBLIC OF CONGO
9 DAHOMEY
10 ETHIOPIA (ABYSSINIA)
11 GABON
12 THE GAMBIA
13 GHANA
14 GUINEA
15 IRAQ
16 IVORY COAST
17 KUWAIT
18 KENYA
19 LESOTHO
20 LIBERIA
21 MADAGASCAR

BAHREIN
Sheikdom
Persian Gulf
Area: 231 sq. miles

Pop: 182,000. **Land use:** mainly desert. **Industries:** petroleum. **Capital:** Manama (79,000).

BOTSWANA* †
Republic
S. Africa
Area: 275,000 sq. miles

Pop: 576,000. **Land use %:** pasture and forest 98; waste 2. **Occupations:** Agricultural (mainly pastoral). **Capital:** Gaberones (12,000).

BURUNDI*
Republic
Central Africa
Area: 11,000 sq. miles

Pop: 3,274,000. **Land use:** mountains and grassland. **Occupations:** agriculture (coffee, hides, skins). **Capital:** Bujumbura (70,000).

CAMEROUN*
Republic
W. Central Africa
Area: 184,000 sq. miles

Pop: 5,550,000. **Land use %:** forest 65; cultivated 18; grassland 11; waste 6. **Occupations:** agriculture. **Capital:** Yaoundé (105,000).

CENTRAL AFRICAN REPUBLIC*
Republic
Central Africa
Area: 236,000 sq. miles

Pop: 2,088,000. **Land use:** forest and savanna grassland. **Occupations:** agriculture (subsistence and plantation), mining. **Industries:** timber. **Capital:** Bangui (83,000).

CHAD*
Republic
North Central Africa
Area: 488,000 sq. miles

Pop: 3,500,000. **Land use:** savanna grassland, desert. **Occupations:** subsistence agriculture, stock raising. **Capital:** Fort Lamy (46,000).

CONGO*
Republic
W. Central Africa
Area: 906,000 sq. miles

Pop: 15,986,000. **Land use %:** forest 42; grassland 37; cultivated 21. **Occupations:** agriculture (plantation crops and subsistence farming), mining. **Capital:** Kinshasa (1,000,000).

REPUBLIC OF CONGO*
Republic
W. Central Africa
Area: 132,000 sq. miles

Pop: 840,000. **Land use:** forest, savanna grassland. **Occupations:** subsistence and plantation agriculture, mining. **Industries:** timber. **Capital:** Brazzaville (136,000).

DAHOMEY*
Republic
W. Africa
Area: 47,000 sq. miles

Pop: 2,410,000. **Land use:** forest and savanna grassland. **Occupations:** subsistence and plantation agriculture. **Capital:** Porto Novo (65,000).

ETHIOPIA (ABYSSINIA)*
Empire
N.E. Africa
Area: 398,000 sq. miles

Pop: 23,000,000. **Land use %:** grassland 53; waste 33; cultivated 10; forest 4. **Occupations:** primitive agriculture. **Capital:** Addis Ababa (449,000).

GABON*
Republic
W. Central Africa
Area: 108,000 sq. miles

Pop: 468,000. **Land use:** forest. **Occupations:** primitive agriculture, mining. **Industries:** timber, petroleum. **Capital:** Libreville (31,000).

THE GAMBIA* †
Constitutional Monarchy
W. Africa
Area: 4,000 sq. miles

Pop: 336,000. **Land use %:** waste (water) 40; forest 39; cultivated 21. **Occupations:** agriculture (subsistence farming and plantations), fishing. **Capital:** Bathurst (28,000).

GHANA* †
Republic
W. Africa
Area: 92,000 sq. miles

Pop: 7,945,000. **Land use %:** forest 52; waste 31; cultivated 17. **Occupations:** agriculture, mining, forestry, fishing. **Capital:** Accra (532,000).

GUINEA*
Republic
W. Africa
Area: 95,000 sq. miles

Pop: 3,608,000. **Land use:** forest, savanna grassland. **Occupations:** agriculture, mining. **Industries:** rubber, iron and bauxite mining. **Capital:** Conakry (120,000).

IRAQ*
Republic
S.W. Asia
Area: 173,000 sq. miles

Pop: 8,262,000. **Land use %:** waste 81; grassland 9; cultivated 6; forest 4. **Occupations:** subsistence agriculture, pastoral. **Industries:** petroleum refining, textiles, crafts. **Capital:** Baghdad (1,008,000).

IVORY COAST*
Republic
W. Africa
Area: 128,000 sq. miles

Pop: 3,835,000. **Land use:** Forest and savanna grassland. **Occupations:** subsistence and plantation agriculture. **Industries:** timber. **Capital:** Abidjan (400,000).

KENYA* †
Republic
E. Africa
Area: 225,000 sq. miles

Pop: 9,643,000. **Land use %:** waste 74; grassland 21; cultivated 3; forest 2. **Occupations:** agriculture, mining, government, transport. **Capital:** Nairobi (330,000).

KUWAIT*
Sheikdom
S.W. Asia
Area: 6,000 sq. miles

Pop: 468,000. **Land use:** mainly desert waste. **Occupations:** primitive agriculture and stock raising. **Industries:** petroleum. **Capital:** Kuwait (100,000).

LESOTHO* †
Kingdom
S. Africa
Area: 12,000 sq. miles

Pop: 976,000. **Land use:** mostly mountains. **Occupations:** agriculture (stock raising). **Capital:** Maseru (9,000).

LIBERIA*
Republic
W. Africa
Area: 43,000 sq. miles

Pop: 1,090,000. **Land use %:** waste 47; forest 35; cultivated 16; grassland 2. **Occupations:** subsistence agriculture, mining. **Industries:** rubber, handicrafts. **Capital:** Monrovia (80,000).

MADAGASCAR*
Republic
Island off S.E. Africa
Area: 229,000 sq. miles

Pop: 6,336,000. **Land use %:** grassland 63; waste 17; forest 12; cultivated 8. **Occupations:** subsistence agriculture, stock raising, mining. **Industries:** handicrafts. **Capital:** Tananarive (322,000).

COUNTRIES OF AFRICA AND ARABIA

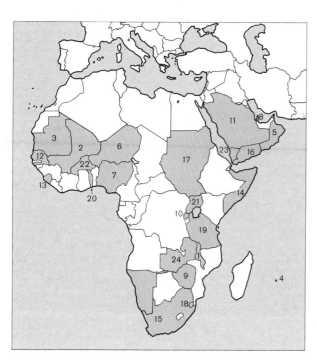

1 MALAWI
2 MALI
3 MAURITANIA
4 MAURITIUS
5 MUSCAT & OMAN
6 NIGER
7 NIGERIA
8 QATAR
9 RHODESIA
10 RWANDA
11 SAUDI ARABIA
12 SENEGAL

13 SIERRA LEONE
14 SOMALIA
15 SOUTH AFRICA
16 SOUTH YEMEN
17 SUDAN
18 SWAZILAND
19 TANZANIA
20 TOGO
21 UGANDA
22 UPPER VOLTA
23 YEMEN
24 ZAMBIA

MAURITANIA*
Republic
N.W. Africa
Area: 419,000 sq. miles

Pop: 1,070,000. **Land use:** savanna grassland, scrub, desert. **Occupations:** stock raising, mining. **Capital:** Nouakchott (15,000).

MAURITIUS* †
Constitutional Monarchy
Indian Ocean
Area: 805 sq. miles

Pop: 768,000. **Land use %:** cultivated 43; grassland 24; forest 19; waste 14. **Occupations:** agriculture (plantation), fishing. **Industry:** processing foodstuffs. **Capital:** Port Louis (134,000).

MUSCAT & OMAN
Sultanate
S.W. Asia
Area: 82,000 sq. miles

Pop: 750,000. **Land use:** mainly desert. **Occupations:** date growing, fishing, petroleum. **Capital:** Muscat (6,000).

NIGER*
Republic
W. Central Africa
Area: 489,000 sq. miles

Pop: 3,433,000. **Land use:** savanna grassland, desert. **Occupations:** stock raising, subsistence agriculture. **Capital:** Niamey (56,000).

NIGERIA* †
Republic
W. Africa
Area: 357,000 sq. miles

Pop: 57,500,000. **Land use %:** waste 49; forest 44; cultivated 7. **Occupations:** agriculture, mining, forestry, government service. **Industries:** mining, petroleum. **Capital:** Lagos (665,000).

QATAR
Sheikdom
S.W. Asia
Area: 4,000 sq. miles

Pop: 60,000. **Land use:** mainly desert waste. **Industries:** petroleum. **Capital:** Doha (45,000).

RHODESIA
U.K. Colony (Internally self-governing)
S.E. Africa
Area: 151,000 sq. miles

Pop: 4,400,000. **Land use:** forest, cultivated, grassland. **Occupations:** forestry, agriculture, mining, fishing, manufacturing. **Industries:** metal products, textiles, chemicals. **Capital:** Salisbury (326,000).

RWANDA*
Republic
Central Africa
Area: 10,000 sq. miles

Pop: 3,000,000. **Land use:** forest, cultivated. **Occupations:** agriculture, some mining. **Capital:** Kigali (7,000).

MALAWI* †
Republic
S.E. Africa
Area: 36,000 sq. miles

Pop: 4,042,000. **Land use:** savanna grassland, some cultivated. **Occupations:** subsistence and plantation agriculture, fishing. **Capital:** Zomba (20,000).

MALI*
Republic
W. Africa
Area: 465,000 sq. miles

Pop: 4,576,000. **Land use:** savanna grassland, forest, desert. **Occupations:** subsistence and plantation agriculture. **Capital:** Bamako (150,000).

SAUDI ARABIA*
Kingdom
S.W. Asia
Area: 927,000 sq. miles

Pop: 8,000,000. **Land use:** mainly desert waste. **Occupations:** primitive agriculture and stock raising. **Industries:** petroleum. **Capital:** Riyadh (170,000).

SENEGAL*
Republic
W. Africa
Area: 76,000 sq. miles.

Pop: 3,490,000. **Land use:** mainly agricultural (groundnuts). **Capital:** Dakar (450,000).

SIERRA LEONE* †
Republic
W. Africa
Area: 28,000 sq. miles

Pop: 2,403,000. **Land use %:** cultivated 56; grassland 30; waste 10; forest 4. **Occupations:** agriculture and mining. **Capital:** Freetown (100,000).

SOMALIA*
Republic
N.E. Africa
Area: 246,000 sq. miles

Pop: 5,000,000. **Land use %:** grassland 58; forest 32; cultivated 8; waste 2. **Occupations:** subsistence agriculture and stock raising. **Capital:** Mogadishu (100,000).

SOUTH AFRICA*
Republic
S. Africa
Area: 472,000 sq. miles

Pop: 18,298,000. **Land use %:** grassland 67; waste 24; cultivated 6; forest 3. **Occupations:** agriculture, forestry, fishing, public services, mining, manufacturing. **Industries:** refining minerals, iron and steel, food processing, clothing and footwear, textiles. **Capitals:** Cape Town (807,000), legislative; Pretoria (423,000), administrative. **Trust territory:** South-West Africa.

SOUTH YEMEN*
Republic
S.W. Asia
Area: 61,000 sq. miles

Pop: 1,250,000. **Land use:** mostly mountains and desert. **Occupations:** subsistence farming. **Industries:** oil refining. **Capital:** Al Ittihad.

SUDAN*
Republic
N.E. and Central Africa
Area: 970,000 sq. miles

Pop: 13,940,000. **Land use %:** waste 52; forest 38; grassland 10. **Occupations:** agriculture. **Capital:** Khartoum (154,000).

SWAZILAND
Kingdom (to become fully independent of U.K. 1969)
S. E. Africa
Area: 7,000 sq. miles

Pop: 389,000. **Land use %:** grassland 78; cultivated 14; waste 7; forest 1. **Occupations:** subsistence agriculture and stock raising, mining. **Capital:** Mbabane (14,000).

TANZANIA* †
Republic (formerly Tanganyika and Zanzibar)
E. Africa
Area: 364,000 sq. miles

Pop: 10,518,000. **Land use %:** forest 42; waste 41; grassland 14; cultivated 3. **Occupations:** agriculture, mining, secondary manufacturing. **Capital:** Dar es Salaam (180,000).

TOGO*
Republic
W. Africa
Area: 22,000 sq. miles

Pop: 1,680,000. **Land use %:** waste 75; cultivated 13; grassland 4; forest 3. **Occupations:** agriculture, stock raising, mining. **Capital:** Lomé (86,000).

UGANDA* †
Republic
E. Africa
Area: 94,000 sq. miles

Pop: 7,740,000. **Land use %:** waste 80; cultivated 12; forest 8. **Occupations:** subsistence agriculture and plantations, mining. **Industries:** metal refining, textiles, cement, foodstuffs. **Capital:** Kampala (12,000).

UPPER VOLTA*
Republic
W. Africa
Area: 106,000 sq. miles

Pop: 4,955,000. **Land use:** savanna grassland, scrub, desert. **Occupations:** stock raising, primitive agriculture. **Capital:** Ouagadougou (100,000).

YEMEN*
Republic
S.W. Arabia
Area: 75,000 sq. miles

Pop: 5,000,000. **Land use:** mainly desert, some cultivation. **Occupations:** subsistence agriculture, stock raising, coffee production. **Capital:** San'a (80,000).

ZAMBIA* †
Republic
S. Central Africa
Area: 290,000 sq. miles

Pop: 3,837,000. **Land use:** some cultivated, forest, scrub. **Occupations:** farming, fishing, mining, some manufacturing. **Capital:** Lusaka (151,000).

* Member of the United Nations
† Member of the British Commonwealth

U.S.S.R. AND EASTERN EUROPE

The U.S.S.R., almost three times as big as the United States, is the largest country in the world. Its vast area is rich in natural resources, and these have helped make it one of the two most powerful countries. After World War II Communist rule was extended to other East European countries, and so they became closely linked with the U.S.S.R.

Forests, Plains and Rivers

If you traveled east by train across the U.S.S.R. from one end to the other, a distance of more than 5,000 miles, you would see almost nothing but monotonous rolling plains. In the south and east high mountains fringe these vast plains where Europe and Asia meet. Crossing the plains from north to south are the Ural Mountains, but they do not exceed 6,000 feet. The plains are not broken up by any real mountain barrier; east-west bands of soil and vegetation, changing with climate, merge imperceptibly into one another.

The Soviet Union is open to cold air from the Arctic and moist air coming from the Atlantic. The north and east are very cold. Oymyakon in northeast Siberia, where a temperature of $-94°$F. was once recorded, is the coldest place in the inhabited world. The south and southeast are dry, except along the Pacific coast, which has a monsoon climate with warm summers and cold, snowy winters.

The most northern zone, bordering the Arctic Ocean, is tundra. This is desolate and mostly flat, although tundra vegetation grows on the upper slopes of the Ural Mountains. Winters are extremely severe with cold, gale force winds. Snow covers the

Russian cathedral in the small village of Bogolyubovo near Vladimir, a town about 125 miles northeast of Moscow. The cathedral was built as part of a fortified palace by the Count of Novgorod between 1158 and 1165. From its position on a hilltop this beautiful Kremlin-in-miniature dominates the low rolling plains of the surrounding landscape.

ground for eight or nine months and the subsoil is always frozen. In summer when the snow melts, a lot of the ground becomes swampy because the water does not drain well.

The next zone, south of the tundra, is the *taiga*. Its enormous forests are mostly coniferous—pine, spruce, fir and larch, together with silver birch. Bears, wolves, elks and other wild animals roam the forests. Fur-bearing animals like the marten and sable have been hunted almost to extinction in Russia and now exist in significant numbers only in Siberia.

Like the tundra, the taiga has few inhabitants because the winters are so long and cold. There was once a mixed forest zone west of the Urals between the taiga and the steppe; but people have lived there for centuries and most of the oaks and other deciduous trees were cut down long ago. Both this zone and the taiga have large patches of swamp or peat bog. You can only travel across the Pripet Marshes of White Russia in winter when both ground and water are frozen.

South of the taiga are the steppes—great rolling plains, treeless except along the banks of the rivers. The soil is fertile black earth, or *chernozem*, and in most areas has been plowed up for wheat growing.

Farther south the landscape changes to semi-desert, where there is sagebrush instead of grass. This in turn gives way to true desert, with shifting sand dunes and salt pans, around the Aral Sea. Here crops are grown only under irrigation and camels are still used for transportation.

West of the Caucasus Mountains and bordering the Black Sea is a warm, damp, subtropical region. Almost frost-free, it has palm trees, eucalyptus and bamboo, and crops like tea and oranges. The Soviet Union's only ice-free winter ports are located on the Black Sea coast.

Great rivers relieve some of the monotony of the Soviet landscape. They include the Volga, Europe's longest river, flowing southwards to the Black Sea; the Ob, Yenisei and Lena, flowing northwards through Siberia; and the Amur, flowing to the Pacific. These rivers are among the longest in the world and are important routeways.

The highest mountains in the Soviet Union are along the southern border. They are the Pamirs, sometimes called "the roof of the world"; their highest mountain, Communism Peak, reaches 24,590 feet. The Tien Shan and other large ranges sprawl out from the Pamirs, separating the Soviet Union from China. Mountains and plateaus run through eastern Siberia and then bend north along the Pacific coast. Lake Baikal (400 miles long), the largest freshwater lake in Asia and the deepest in the world, is set in these mountains.

The rugged Caucasus Mountains, between the Soviet Union and Turkey, also have many high peaks. Mount Elbrus (18,481 feet) is the highest mountain in Europe. Sweeping in a huge arc from Poland to Rumania, through the southwest corner of the Soviet Union, are the Carpathians. Although they are an extension of the Alpine system, the Carpathians are a lot lower. With the mountains of Bohemia they lie at the southern edge of the North European Plain, which extends across East Germany and Poland and slopes gently down to the Baltic. Within the curve of the Carpathians lie the Hungarian Plain and the plain of the lower Danube. The Balkan Mountains, backbone of Bulgaria, run eastwards parallel with the Danube River.

Top left: mountaineering in the Caucasus. The main ranges, stretching 750 miles from the Taman Peninsula on the Black Sea to Apsheron Peninsula on the Caspian, have many impressive peaks including Mount Elbrus (18,481 feet).
Top right: a typical landscape in the Ukraine, southwest Russia. In summer the black earth is covered with a sea of wheat sometimes stretching to the horizon and only broken by the trees planted as windbreaks or around the scattered houses for summer shade and winter shelter.

Left: Dikson Island, a port and weather station at the mouth of the Yenisei River and on the northern sea route between Murmansk and Vladivostok. This route is open to shipping only during the brief Arctic summer.
Right: the Kara Kum Canal. This takes water from the Amu-Darya River through the barren southern Kara Kum Desert to the Mary Oasis where the land has been irrigated for hundreds of years. There is now an 86-mile long extension to Tedzhen.

Agriculture and Fisheries

Bulgaria grows roses not for their beauty but to make attar of roses, a valuable oil used in perfumery. The main growing area is between Rozino and Sliven in the sheltered valley of the upper Tundzha River, and its distillery is at Kazanluk. Increasing competition from synthetic perfumes threatens the industry.

Harvesting on the Veselovsky State Farm in the Rostov region of the Soviet Union. More than 17,290 acres are sown with cereals on this farm every year and the yield per acre is gradually increasing with the use of new chemical fertilizers.

In spite of the importance of industry and the drift of people to the towns and cities, about a third of the Soviet Union's labor force still works on the land. Agricultural production has increased—the U.S.S.R. leads the world in wheat and rye production—but farm yields cannot yet meet the growing demand for food. Recently there has been a grain shortage and vast quantities have been imported, especially from Canada, the United States and Australia.

In the U.S.S.R. all land is owned by the state. Soviet farms are completely different from the farms of North America. There are two kinds: *collective* and *state*. On collective farms *(kolkhozy)* the workers use machinery, fertilizers and seed provided by the state. Production is planned by the state and the workers receive a share of farm profits instead of a regular paycheck. Each household has a small patch of land, not more than four acres, for private use. Workers on state farms *(Sovkhozy)* are government employees so they are paid salaries. They, too, have their own small patches of land.

Both state and collective farms cover huge tracts of land, sometimes as much as 100,000 acres. This makes large-scale use of machinery possible, and mechanization cuts farming costs. Mechanization is on the increase, but transportation of agricultural produce is still difficult. Many farms are a long way from towns and railroads, and the country dirt roads are often impassable just when the crops have to be harvested.

After World War II East European governments set up state and collective farms. By 1960, East German agriculture was completely collectivized. In Poland and, to a lesser extent, Czechoslovakia collectivization was unpopular. So many collectives were broken up again in small private units. But in Poland "agricultural groups" have recently been formed and this may be a return to partial collectivization.

Large areas of the U.S.S.R. are good farmland, especially the "Fertile Triangle" between Leningrad, Odessa and Lake Baikal. The most important part of the triangle is the steppe zone with its rich black soils. Main crops here are wheat, sugar beet, sunflowers, barley, potatoes and corn. North from the steppes, where it is wetter and cooler, the main crops include barley, flax and hemp; and dairy farming is also important. Rye is grown in the northwest.

Farmers in the irrigated areas of Central Asia outside the Fertile Triangle grow cotton. Many irrigation canals cross this dry region. The Kara Kum Canal from the river Amu-Darya to the Mary

Cotton harvesting in the warm, well-watered lands of the Ferghana Valley, Uzbekistan, where the intensive farming is based on irrigation. Farmers in this region of Central Asia, Russia's chief cotton growing area, also produce fruit, silk and rice.

Logs awaiting transportation to the timber mills. Nearly 40 per cent of the Soviet Union is forested; the northern coniferous forests are the largest. These vast resources make the U.S.S.R. the world's leading timber producer.

Oasis is one of the largest. Tea, citrus fruits and tobacco grow in the subtropical region of the Trans-Caucasus.

The Soviet Union is vast, but a lot of land is not suitable for agriculture. Deserts and mountains in the south and east and short, cool summers in the north make farming impossible. But the Soviet Government is constantly seeking new ways of increasing food production. The ambitious Virgin Lands project in western Siberia and Kazakhstan involved plowing great tracts of new land for grain growing. But this region has the disadvantage of a very low annual rainfall. The land must be farmed carefully to avoid dustbowl conditions. Long forest belts are often planted to reduce damage from the great dust storms that sometimes sweep the U.S.S.R.

The seas, rivers and lakes of the U.S.S.R. are valuable fishing grounds. Soviet fishing fleets, using the most modern techniques, operate in all the seas around the Soviet Union, even the inland seas (Caspian and Aral). Whaling fleets also sail from Odessa to the Antarctic every year.

The Soviet Union is the world's leading producer of timber, with forests over one third of her land area. The northern forests of Karelia, the Archangelsk region and Siberia are the most important. Logs are often floated downstream to northern ports like Archangel and Igarka, or south down the Volga to the industrial centers. Loading timber at the northern ports begins in July and continues through September, but no later because ships using the Northern Sea Route must leave the Arctic before the ports become icebound.

Both Czechoslovakia and Poland have large forests. Czechoslovakia is one of the most heavily forested countries in Europe. About 30 per cent of Bulgaria and 25 per cent of Rumania are covered by forests of oak, beech and conifers, and forestry is an important industry, providing timber for homes and pulp for paper making. Hungary has only small forests and so has to import timber.

Mineral Resources and Industry

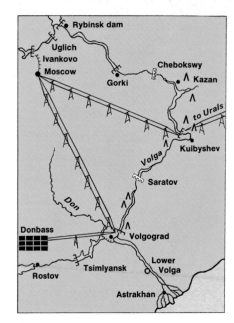

Legend

🕸 High tension lines

∧ Oil fields

▬ Coal fields

⊓ Dams

ᴍ Dams under construction

ᴜ Canals

○ Possible new dam

Industrial map of the Volga and Don River basins. The Volga and its tributaries carry two thirds of all the river traffic in the U.S.S.R.

The transformation of a sprawling, predominantly agricultural country into the world's second strongest industrial power is one of the most remarkable features of the Soviet Union. Industrialization came much later to the U.S.S.R. than it did to Northwest Europe or the United States. The beginning was made in 1928 when the Soviet Government initiated a series of Five Year Plans for economic development. These plans were prepared by the Gosplan (State Planning Commission).

Each plan set targets for increased agricultural and industrial production, and scheduled the opening of new mines and factories. In every plan heavy industry had priority. The third Five Year Plan was cut short by World War II, and the sixth was interrupted and replaced by a Seven Year Plan which ended in 1965. The current Five Year Plan ends in 1971.

Underlying economic development is a basic fact of the Soviet system: all natural resources, mines and factories are owned by the state. There is no private enterprise; there are no large corporations. Each major industry is the responsibility of its own government ministry.

The U.S.S.R. has immense resources. With more than half the world's reserves, the Soviet Union leads the world in coal production and her mines are almost fully mechanized. The major fields are the Donbas (short for Donetz Basin) in the Ukraine, the Kuzbas (Kuznets Basin) in Siberia, Karaganda in Central Asia and Vorkuta near the Arctic coast. In Eastern Europe both Poland and East Germany are important coal producers. Poland has the Upper Silesian coal basin; East Germany the Saxony coalfield. East Germany is the world's leading producer of lignite (brown coal), often used for firing power stations. The chief Hungarian coalfields are near Pécs and Komlo. Bulgaria has the Balkanbas, a coalfield south of Gabrovo and Elena. Czechoslovakia mines coal at Most, Chomutov, Kladno, Ostrava and Sokolov.

The Soviet Union has large oilfields near the Caucasus, especially around Baku; some of the wells are 20 miles offshore in the Caspian Sea. Other Caucasian oilfields are centered on Grozny and Maikop. A "second Baku" has been developed in the Ural-Volga area and yet another oilfield in the Trans-Volga area of the Saratov region. There is also a smaller field on the island of Sakhalin, off the Pacific coast. The Soviet Union is second only to the United States in oil production. Some Soviet oil is piped to East European countries. Rumania has an oilfield northwest of Ploesti at the southern tip of the Carpathians. Bulgaria has some oil in the Balchik area on the Black Sea coast.

Some of the world's largest hydroelectric power plants are in the U.S.S.R., and all of them are fully automatic. The map shows those on the Volga River. There are also large dams on other rivers—for example, at Dnepropetrovsk on the Dniepr and at Bratsk on the Angara (the world's largest power station). There are plans for a large new hydroelectric plant on the Danube between Gura Vaii (Rumania) and Sip (Yugoslavia), due for completion by 1970.

The hydro-electric power project on the Angara River at Bratsk, Siberia, during construction. This project, the world's largest hydro-electric plant, has a dam 400 feet high, a reservoir 350 miles long and a 4.5 million kilowatt capacity. It came into operation in 1967. Iron ore deposits near Bratsk form the basis of the town's industry.

Automated production line at a diesel engine plant in Kharkov, in the Ukraine. Kharkov's industry is based on Donbas coal and iron ore from Krivoi Rog. Its products include locomotives, and turbines. Its population of 1,125,000 makes Kharkov one of the largest cities in the Soviet Union.

The Soviet Union leads the world in iron ore production. The Urals have more than 1,000 minerals, many in workable deposits. Manganese, chrome, molybdenum, copper, gold, platinum, mercury and bauxite are mined on a large scale. In Eastern Europe, mineral resources are smaller, but the bauxite of Hungary and the iron ore of Poland are important. Poland also has Europe's most unusual mines. These are the rock salt mines at Wieliczka, which have been worked since the 11th century. They are at 7 different levels and contain two chapels carved from the natural rock.

Heavy industry is naturally centered mainly near the coalfields and raw materials. Some industrial towns have grown from nothing, like Magnitogorsk in the south Urals, an iron and steel center; Nowa Huta (Poland) and Dunaujvaros (Hungary), both steel towns; Dmitrovgrad (Bulgaria), with its large chemical works. Two important older manufacturing areas in the U.S.S.R. are around Moscow and Leningrad. These areas have no local sources of raw materials so they specialize in textiles, auto-mobiles, high grade precision products, electrical and electronic equipment and machine tools. The Soviet government is promoting industrial dispersal, partly to bring industries nearer raw materials and the markets for their finished goods, partly because large concentrations of industry are vulnerable targets for atomic bombs.

In both Eastern Europe and the U.S.S.R. railroads are an important form of transportation. The most famous, the 5,800 mile-long Trans-Siberian, goes right across the Soviet Union from Moscow to the Pacific coast. Many lines have been electrified and diesel locomotives are taking over from steam. Compared with the United States, however, the Soviet Union has few railroads and highways. Dirt roads, often impassable in wet weather, are common in the countryside. Airlines serve the main centers and link them with the more remote places in the Arctic and in Central Asia. There are many canals. Moscow, because of its canal and river routes, is sometimes called the "port of the five seas" (Baltic, White, Caspian, Azov and Black Sea).

Top: May Day and the anniversary of the October Revolution (November 7) are celebrated with impressive military and civilian parades in Moscow centered on the Red Square and the Kremlin or citadel (left). The Kremlin contains three cathedrals and several palaces, including the Palace of the Supreme Soviet, where the Chamber of Deputies and Chamber of Nationalities meet.

Below: Uzbek girls wearing their national costume. The Soviet Government encourages the cultures of individual racial groups and the Uzbeks are just one of the many nationalities of the U.S.S.R. which still preserve their own language, customs, and folk dress.

The Soviet Union is three times the size of the United States and has a population of about 235 million made up of many different nationalities. The census of 1959 listed 108 different national groups. Each major group has its own Union Republic.

The Russians make up more than half the population; most live in the R.S.F.S.R. (Russian Soviet Federated Socialist Republic). The next largest groups are the Ukrainians and the White Russians. Other groups large enough to have their own Republics are the Georgians, Azerbaidzhanis and Armenians in the Caucasus; the Uzbeks, Kazahks, Tadzhiks, Kirgiz and Turkmenians of Central Asia; the Estonians (related to the Finns), Latvians and Lithuanians; and the Moldavians on the Rumanian frontier.

Smaller groups, like the Tartars (who almost conquered all of Russia 600 years ago), are scattered over the U.S.S.R. Some live in "Autonomous Republics" or "Autonomous Regions" and some in "National Areas". In the far north there are tribes like the Yakuts, who ride reindeer, the Eskimos and Chukchi, who still live as nomadic hunters and herdsmen. The Soviet Government is gradually settling them in permanent communities. While Russian is the official language, the Government encourages national groups to preserve their languages and cultures.

The focal point of the Soviet Union and its largest city is Moscow, which has a population of 6½ million, swollen daily by a million commuters and visitors. Leningrad, the second largest city, has a population of 3¾ million. More than half the population of the Soviet Union now lives in towns and cities. This is due not only to a general drift to urban areas, but to the rapid development of new cities, especially in the eastern parts of the country.

Housing is a problem in most towns and cities: you have to get a permit to live in Moscow or Leningrad. Often more than one family shares an apartment, but rents are low by Western standards.

Women have a special place in Soviet Society.

Budapest, the Hungarian capital, by night. On the hilly western bank (left) of the Danube the old city of Buda clusters round its fortress. On the low eastern bank is modern Pest. Budapest and other cities along the Danube's 1,800-mile course to the Black Sea are busy river ports.

They outnumber men by more than 20 million, chiefly because of the terrible casualties in World War II. They are a vital part of the labor force, and even do heavy work on construction sites and truck driving. There are special day nurseries to look after children while their mothers are at work.

The Government gives education high priority. Schooling, which is free, may begin with nursery school at the age of three, and leads on to the universities, colleges and technical training institutes. The largest is Moscow State University, with about 16,000 students. Most students receive a government grant towards living expenses, but they have to work two years on a farm or in a factory before they can go to college. Emphasis is on science and technology, but literature and the arts still have an honored place.

The Poles, Czechs, Slovaks and Bulgars of Eastern Europe are all Slavs. Their relationship to the Russians and Ukrainians shows in their languages, which have many similarities. Their cultures, however, have been influenced greatly by western Europe. The Germans were once scattered throughout Eastern Europe. Now most of them have returned to Germany, although there are still more than 1 ½ million people of German descent living in the Soviet Union. The Hungarian Magyars speak a language distantly related to Finnish. The Rumanian language is derived from Latin and is not unlike Italian.

The Bulgarian language is of slavonic origin and is closely related to Russian. (The alphabet is Cyrillic.) But Bulgarian also has words derived from Greek, Albanian and Turkish.

Moscow University students reading a wall newspaper. Russian newspapers like *Pravda* and *Izvestia*, faithful mirrors of official policy, appear on walls everywhere—in offices, factories, universities and in the streets—so that all may know the line they are required to take.

Top: Russian leaders take the salute at a Moscow parade. Left to right: Marshal Grechko, Marshal Voroshilov, Marshal Malinovsky, L. I. Brezhnev (First Secretary of the Communist Party), Alexei Kosygin (Chairman of the Council of Ministers), Nikolai Podgorny (President), M. A. Suslov and A. I. Mikoyan (Members of the Presidium).
Bottom: lecture on artificial earth satellites (sputniks) at the Moscow Planetarium. Russia's Academy of Sciences is in Moscow.

U.S.S.R., Eastern Europe and the World

Its size and population, its resources and development, and the relentless political philosophy which drives it, make the Soviet Union one of the world's most powerful countries.

The Soviet Union heads the Eastern European Communist bloc (Bulgaria, Czechoslovakia, East Germany, Hungary, Poland and Rumania). Albania, also a Communist state, has been a faithful follower of Communist China in recent years. And Yugoslavia, another Communist country, holds a more independent position between the Communist bloc and the West, but retains close associations with Moscow. More recently the Communist countries of Eastern Europe generally have adopted more independent attitudes from time to time.

Communist unity is seen clearly in defense policy and economic development. The Eastern Security Treaty (Warsaw Pact), signed in 1955 by the U.S.S.R., Albania, Bulgaria, Czechoslovakia, East Germany, Hungary, Poland and Rumania, is virtually the Communist equivalent of the North Atlantic Treaty. The Council for Mutual Economic Aid, known in the West as COMECON, was established in 1949 to integrate the economies of the Communist countries. Its members include the U.S.S.R., East European countries and Mongolia. Albania withdrew in 1961. Communist China, North Korea and North Vietnam are represented by observers.

The Russians have a long tradition of scientific research. This tradition has been continued and enriched by present-day scientists and technologists in the Soviet Union. The launching of the first artificial satellite and the first manned flight in space are only two of many recent achievements.

Such demonstrations of expertise and power are formidable prestige builders for the Soviet Union. In the United Nations, where the U.S.S.R. is a permanent member of the Security Council and so has power of veto, and elsewhere in world affairs, Russian views and attitudes inevitably command constant attention.

72

1 BULGARIA
2 CZECHOSLOVAKIA
3 GERMANY (EAST)
4 HUNGARY
5 POLAND
6 RUMANIA
7 UNION OF SOVIET
  SOCIALIST REPUBLICS

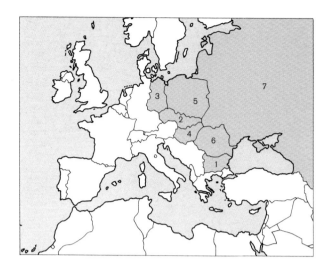

COUNTRIES OF
EASTERN EUROPE

BULGARIA*
Republic
S.E. Europe
Area: 43,000 sq. miles

Pop: 8,258,000. **Land use** %: cultivated 39; forest 33; waste 26; meadow and pasture 2. **Occupations:** agriculture (75%), industry; **Industries:** heavy industry, chemicals, oil, textile manufacture increasing. **Capital:** Sofia (828,000).

CZECHOSLOVAKIA*
Republic
Central Europe
Area: 49,000 sq. miles

Pop: 14,272,000. **Land use** %: arable 44; forest 32; grassland 16; waste 8. **Occupations:** agriculture, manufacturing, professions. **Industries:** iron and steel, engineering, locomotives and automobiles, textiles, glass. **Capital:** Prague (1,025,000).

GERMANY (EAST)
Republic
N. Europe
Area: 42,000 sq. miles

Pop: 17,067,000. **Land use** %: cultivated 47; forest 28; waste 13; meadow and pasture 12. **Occupations:** agriculture, mining, communications, trade, manufacturing. **Industries:** textiles, machinery, precision instruments, heavy engineering. **Capital:** East Berlin (1,200,000).

HUNGARY*
Republic
Central Europe
Area: 36,000 sq. miles

Pop: 10,179,000. **Land use** %: arable 62; grassland 17; forest 12; waste 9. **Occupations:** agriculture, manufacturing. **Industries:** iron and steel, heavy engineering, textiles, food processing. **Capital:** Budapest (1,952,000).

POLAND*
Republic
E. Europe
Area: 121,000 sq. miles

Pop: 31,711,000. **Land use** %: arable 54; forest 22; grassland 13; waste 11. **Occupations:** agriculture, manufacturing, mining. **Industries:** iron and steel, coal, engineering, textiles, food processing. **Capital:** Warsaw (1,249,000).

RUMANIA*
Republic
S.E. Europe
Area: 92,000 sq. miles

Pop: 19,150,000. **Land use** %: arable 39; forest 28; waste 19; grassland 14. **Occupations:** agriculture, manufacturing, mining. **Industries:** petroleum, refining, coal, timber. **Capital:** Bucharest (1,511,000).

UNION OF SOVIET
SOCIALIST REPUBLICS*
Republic
Eurasia
Area: 8,647,000 sq. miles

Pop: 235,500,000. **Land use** %: waste 43; forest 41; cultivated 10; grassland 6. **Occupations:** agriculture, industry, building and construction, mining. **Industries:** iron and steel, heavy engineering, atomic power, aircraft, automobiles, electrical equipment, timber, etc. **Capital:** Moscow (6,507,000). **Largest cities:** Moscow, Leningrad (3,706,000), Kiev (1,413,000), Tashkent (1,241,000) Baku (1,196,000), Kharkov (1,125,000).

REPUBLIC	AREA (sq. miles)	POPULATION	CAPITAL
Russian Soviet Federal Socialist Republic (RSFSR)	6,593,000	127,312,000	Moscow
Ukraine*	232,000	45,966,000	Kiev
Byelorussia*	80,000	8,744,000	Minsk
Uzbekistan	158,000	10,896,000	Tashkent
Kazakhstan	1,064,000	12,413,000	Alma-Ata
Georgia	26,000	4,611,000	Tbilisi
Azerbaijan	33,000	4,802,000	Baku
Lithuania	26,000	3,026,000	Vilnius
Moldavia	13,000	3,425,000	Kishinev
Latvia	25,000	2,285,000	Riga
Kirghizia	77,000	2,740,000	Frunze
Tadzhikistan	54,000	2,654,000	Dushanbe
Armenia	11,000	2,253,000	Erevan
Turkmenistan	188,000	1,971,000	Ashkhabad
Estonia	17,000	1,294,000	Tallinn

* Member of the United Nations

The Himalayas cover most of Nepal. On the border with Tibet is Mount Everest, the world's highest mountain. In the south the Himalayas descend to the *Terai* (marshy plain and jungle). The mountain slopes are fertile.

INDIA AND THE FAR EAST

South of the U.S.S.R., Asia spreads out from high plateaus and lofty mountains, across the scrub and desert belt that stretches from Iran through Mongolia, to the monsoon lands of the southeast and the island fringe beyond. Only one tenth of the total land area is low and flat, but it is in this tenth that 90 per cent of the people live.

Subcontinent of India

Shut off from the rest of Asia by lofty mountains and deep valleys, the vast subcontinent of India thrusts southwards like a great wedge between the Arabian Sea and the Bay of Bengal. The distance from the mountain barrier in the north to Ceylon in the south is 2,000 miles; from Karachi in the west to Assam in the east is also about 2,000 miles. The subcontinent is larger than Europe and it is one of the world's most populous areas. Its three main regions, going south to north, are the Deccan (sometimes called Peninsular India), the Indo-Gangetic Plains, and the high mountain wall of the Himalayas and other ranges.

The Deccan is a large plateau sloping down to the southeast from a rugged and well-forested mountain range, the Western Ghats. There is only a narrow coastal plain between this range and the Arabian Sea. In the east, between 50 and 150 miles from the coast is another range, the Eastern Ghats, cut by a series of broad river valleys into a broken line of hills. The Nilgiri Hills, which have an average height of 6,500 feet, are a southern extension of the Western Ghats.

The flat, monotonous Indo-Gangetic Plains stretch across northern India from the Arabian Sea to the Bay of Bengal to the north of the Deccan.

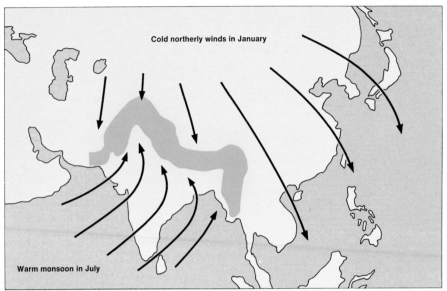

Cold northerly winds in January

Warm monsoon in July

Map illustrating the climatic effect produced by the mountains separating Central Asia from the Indian subcontinent. In July the mountains prevent the moist warm air of the southwest monsoon from reaching Central Asia, while in January they protect India from the cold northerly winds.

Porters negotiating a difficult part of the main trade route through the deep, steep-sided Arun Valley in east Nepal. In the Himalayas roads are few and in some parts all loads have to be carried by porters since the going is too rough even for animals.

Their average width is 250 miles. Three great rivers—Indus, Ganges and Brahmaputra—flow down from the mountains and cross the plains. The land level is gradually rising because the three rivers deposit millions of tons of debris on the plains every year. Most of India's cotton, and large crops of wheat and sugar cane, are grown in this fertile alluvial soil.

There is a striking contrast between the western and eastern parts of the plains. In the west are dry lands; less than 10 inches of rain a year falls on the Thar Desert. So farmers irrigate their land with water from the Indus and its tributaries. They take so much water that in places the Indus is only a small stream. Houses in the dry lands are made of mud brick and have flat roofs. Farther east there is more rain; the houses are still made of mud, but have straw or bamboo roofs, pitched steeply so rain water will run off.

The third region, the lofty mountain wall, has many gigantic peaks reaching heights of more than 20,000 feet. Mount Everest (29,028 feet) is the highest mountain in the world. Through history the mountain valleys of the northwest have been corridors for invasions of India. The only really great gap in the mountains is the Khyber Pass, which links the Indian subcontinent with the Eurasian steppes. It is controlled by Afghanistan.

Both Afghanistan and Iran are dry, mountainous and rocky. There is little cultivation, except in small irrigated plains and valleys, but there are vast tracts of poor grazing land.

The Himalayas are really a succession of parallel ranges, which include the Karakoram range and the Hindu Kush. In winter these mountains protect India from the cold winds of Central Asia; in

Treadmill-type water wheel still widely used for irrigation in India. Most farms are small, the methods inefficient and the equipment primitive. Efforts are being made to educate the farmers and improve production. Agriculture provides work for about 70 per cent of the population.

summer they prevent the wet monsoon from reaching Central Asia. So winters in northern India are much warmer than those of southern China at the same latitudes.

Most of the subcontinent has a tropical monsoon climate. There are three seasons: cool, hot and dry, and rainy. The cool season lasts from October to February; the northeast monsoon blows and the weather is mild and dry; the northern plains may even get some frost. From March until early June the winds are still from the northeast, but it is hot and dry. On the Indo-Gangetic Plains temperatures often rise over 100°F. Then atmospheric pressure changes over the Indian Ocean and winds blow from the southwest. From the beginning of June the weather is muggy and hot, since the warm, moist air from the Indian Ocean cannot rise above the layer of calm, warm air at about 12,000 feet. Suddenly, about mid-June, there is a change. The layer of calm air slips away north and the warm moist air rises and cools. The monsoon breaks with torrential rain, especially heavy on the Western Ghats and the Assam Hills.

In Ceylon it is hot all year. The southwest monsoon brings heavy rain to the south and southwest in summer; the northeast monsoon brings rain to the northeast in winter.

The island of Ceylon, which is separated from the southeast tip of India by Palk Strait and the Gulf of Manaar, is a little larger than West Virginia. Most of the island is undulating plain, but the south has central mountains reaching heights of more than 6,000 feet. The highest is Pidurutallagalla, or Pedrotallagalla (known locally as Pedro); from its summit (8,291 feet) the entire coastline of Ceylon can be seen on a clear day. The most famous is Adam's Peak (7,360 feet). The natural hollow at its summit, resembling a giant footprint, is said by Buddhists to have been made by the Buddha, and by Hindus to be the footprint of Siva. The Chinese say that it was made by Pan Ku, their own first man.

Giant bamboos in Peradeniya Botanical Gardens near Kandy, Ceylon. This country is hot all year round and vegetation in the island's extremely wet highlands grows to tremendous heights.

Southeast Asian Countries

Left: trained elephants are used as forest workers in Burma hauling large logs to the river where they can be floated downstream to the sawmills at Rangoon, Moulmein and other centers. Timber, especially teak and other hardwoods, is one of Burma's chief exports.

Southeast Asia, a region of mountains, plains and islands lies between India, China and Australia. A complex patchwork quilt of countries and landscapes, it includes the peninsula of Indochina and the islands of the East Indies and the Philippines.

Within Southeast Asia there are two systems of fold mountains. The Philippine mountains rise abruptly from great ocean deeps and form a festoon of islands. They belong to a system that stretches right from Australia north through the islands off the east coast of Asia. The second broken chain runs west from the islands of the Banda Sea, through Java and Sumatra. You can trace the range as it curves north through the Nicobar and Andaman Islands where it links up with the Arakan Yoma Mountains just west of the Irrawaddy River. The Arakan Yoma range is one of several spread out like fingers from the eastern end of the Tibetan Plateau and Himalayan range.

Areas of stress and strain in the earth's crust coincide with the lines of fold mountains. Volcanoes and earthquake centers lie along lines of weakness and both the East Indies and the Philippines have active volcanoes. Volcanic material is sometimes acid and does not weather down into good soil. But the volcanic material on Java is not acid and has worn away to form extremely fertile soil.

The region's rivers (especially the mainland streams) have built huge alluvial plains and are still pushing deltas out into the sea. The rivers carry loads of debris down from the mountains and flood easily, depositing silt on the plains. Most of the Indonesian islands have patches of alluvial plain along the coast and these scattered lowlands support large populations. In Sumatra the lowland is continuous along the northern shore. Celebes (now called Sulawesi) has only scattered lowlands. Mangrove swamps in low coastal regions are also gradually extending the land out to sea. Mangroves grow in shallow coastal water. Their long, arching roots anchor the trees and at the same time form an impenetrable barrier that traps soil.

Both the East Indies and the Malay Peninsula

Paddy fields in a hilly region have to be divided into tiny plots separated by low banks. This enables the farmer to keep the same water level in each plot. When the seed heads develop the water is drained off to concentrate the growth in the grain.

The unusual houses of the Bataks who live in a remote part of northern Sumatra, Indonesia. The houses are decorated with intricate carving and the roofs have a steep pitch to cope with the very heavy tropical rainfall.

are equatorial. The weather is always hot, heavy rain falls all year and the air is always humid. This kind of climate produces equatorial rain forest and similar conditions to those of the Congo Basin in Africa.

Indochina and the Philippines have a tropical monsoon climate. In Indochina, summers are hot and rainy like India's. But since the Philippines are islands, the heaviest rain comes in the cool season and is brought by the northeast monsoon. This wind also brings most of the rain to the east coast of Indochina. Tropical monsoon forest, full of deciduous trees like teak, is the natural vegetation in this area.

Plantation growers have cleared the natural vegetation from Southeast Asia and used the land for commercial crops. These are the extensive rubber plantations introduced at the end of the nineteenth century by Europeans. Tea, sugar and spices like cinchona (for quinine) grow on plantations in the East Indies, which were once called "the Spice Islands".

As in all monsoon countries, rice is a major food crop in Southeast Asia. In the growing season rice needs water several inches deep. On the Irrawaddy Delta the water comes from the heavy local rainfall. Farmers in the Philippines grow rice on irrigated terraces, often high up the mountainside. Some of the terraces on the island of Luzon were made thousands of years ago and cultivated continuously down through the centuries.

The floating market in Bangkok, the capital and largest city of Thailand (Siam). The city lies on the delta of the Chao Phraya River and is intersected by waterways, canals (*klongs*) and dikes, but is well served by modern roads. Its buildings include the impressive Wat Phra Keo (page 92). Bangkok is the chief port and communications center of Thailand.

This present-day Mongol herdsman might have been the artist's model for the 13th century rock engraving (top right). The Mongols are still mainly herdsmen, moving from pasture to pasture with their horses, camels, cattle, sheep and goats, and living in wood-frame felt tents. But industry is being developed at Ulan Bator, the capital of Mongolia.

You could put all of the United States into China and still have room to spare. Mongolia could comfortably take the whole of Alaska. Together, Mongolia and China extend across 49 degrees of longitude and 62 degrees of latitude; from the 6,000-mile monsoon coastlands of China far into Central Asia, and from the mountain barriers of the southwest to the Mongolian Plateau and Manchuria in the north.

Great mountains and high plateaus make up about four fifths of this vast area, but here are also broad plains and long rivers that flow mostly from west to east, for China generally slopes eastward from the Tibetan Plateau to the China Seas.

The chief plains are the Middle and Lower Yangtze Plain, the North China Plain and the Manchurian Plain; each of these is about the same area (116,000 square miles—nearly twice the size of Michigan). Other smaller but important lowlands are the Si-Kiang delta and the Chengtu Plain in Szechwan. All these lowlands are intensively cultivated.

China's great rivers have built these broad alluvial plains quite recently in geological history and the process is still going on. The rivers are pushing the coastline out into the sea. The Hwang-ho, for instance, deposits about 1,400 tons of silt every year off the China coast. In the Yangtze valley 5,000 years ago, the coastline was about halfway between Shanghai and Nanking. The North China Plain was once a shallow sea separating the mountains of the Shantung Peninsula from the mainland; today you could bore down 3,000 feet and still not reach solid rock, since old marine sands and gravels are covered by a deep layer of river alluvium.

The Loess Highlands, between the Great Wall of China and the Tsinling Shan, make this one of the most fertile areas in the country. Here, too, are some of China's largest cities like Peking, the capital, and Mukden and Harbin. A great build-up of fine fertile loam, hundreds of feet deep, has buried most of the older landscape. It was probably deposited about 10,000 to 20,000 years ago, at the end of the last Ice Age, by winds blowing from the Gobi Desert. (North China still experiences great dust storms.) Through the loess the rivers have cut steepsided gorges. The Hwang River gets its murky yellow color from the mud it carries downstream from the Loess Highlands. This river has been called "China's sorrow" since it often floods the North China Plain.

The great Plateau of Mongolia lies to the north of the Loess Highlands. Dry and windswept, covered with steppe grasses, it stretches from Sinkiang in the west to Manchuria in the northeast. In the south is the desolate Gobi Desert, partly sand and partly stone, but mostly dry steppe. It has an area of about 500,000 square miles. Crossed by ancient trade routes, including the famous "Silk Road" between China and India, the Gobi Desert is the home of Mongol nomads, wild horses and wild camels.

West of the Yangtze Plains rugged uplands and hills surround the Szechwan Basin. Rivers cut through the hills and the Basin has good farm land.

Southern China is almost separated from the north by the Tsinling Shan and other mountains

reaching out nearly to the mouth of the Yangtze. Here the Kwangsi, Kweichow and Yunnan Plateaus rise in three great steps to the massive Plateau of Tibet. Standing at an average altitude of 15,000 feet, this plateau embraces nearly all of Asia's highest lands. On its southern edge rise the great Himalayan ranges; on its northern, the Kunlun Shan. There are many massive peaks in the Kunlun Shan, but the highest is Ulugh Muztagh (25,340 feet) at the closely folded western end of this mountain chain.

Between the Kunlun Shan and the Altai Mountains in Mongolia are the Takla Makan Desert and the Dzungarian Basin. Parts of the Takla Makan are fertile; but despite the many oases, the desert is generally uninhabitable. Large areas are just shifting sand dunes. The Turfan Depression, 500 feet below sea level, lies to the north of the Takla Makan; here archaeologists have found traces of a civilization nearly 2,000 years old. To the west the border between China and the Soviet Union is dominated by the Tien Shan range. Tengri Khan, its highest peak, towers to 23,616 feet.

An area so vast as Mongolia and China has naturally great variations in climate. The main factors are the monsoon winds, bringing warm, moist air from the sea during summer, and cold, dry air from Central Asia during winter. Their influence is, of course, modified by latitude, altitude and distance from the sea. For example, the summer monsoons coming in from the sea meet their first barrier in the Nanling mountains and their extensions; so the southeast has a rainfall of between 60 and 80 inches a year. After each succeeding range the rainfall decreases until there is virtually no rain at all. On the edge of the Gobi Desert there is less than 2 inches a year.

In summer, places in the north may be just as warm, or even warmer, than places in the south. In winter, the north is bitterly cold, but parts of the south will be very mild. In the Gobi Desert the variation is extreme: as much as 100°F. in summer but less than −30°F. in winter.

Korea and Japan

Top: rush hour in Tokyo, Japan's capital. More than 13 million people live in Tokyo, one of the largest cities in the world. It stands on the Sumida River on the east coast of Honshu Island.
Below: Shinto priests at Kyoto. Although Shinto (the Way of the Gods) ceased to be the state religion of Japan in 1946, it still has nearly 80 million adherents.

By American or Asian standards, both Korea and Japan are small countries. Korea, a peninsula jutting out towards the Japanese island of Kyushu, is slightly larger than Kansas; it is divided politically into North and South Korea along the 38th parallel of latitude. Japan, a country of islands, is slightly smaller than Montana but larger than all of Germany.

In the north, Korea is almost cut off from the rest of Asia by mountains. Rugged mountains stretch all along the east coast too. In some places there are narrow patches of coastal plain; in others the mountains rise straight out of the sea. Most rivers flow west and south from the mountains across broad plains to the Yellow Sea. An island-studded strait 110 miles wide divides Korea from Japan and links the deep Sea of Japan with the shallow Sea of China.

Japan has four main islands—Honshu, Hokkaido, Kyushu and Shikoku, in order of size—and hundreds of smaller islands. They extend in a gentle arc about 1,500 miles from southwest to northeast. Mountains cover about six sevenths of the country and there is only a little farmland, but this is cultivated intensively. The mountains are part of the broken chain that runs from the Philippines and Formosa (Taiwan) to the Kamchatka Peninsula of the Soviet Union.

Japan is a beautiful country. Its islands are the tops of mountains rising seven or eight miles from the floor of the Pacific. On Honshu the Japanese Alps have many peaks over 10,000 feet high, including Mount Fuji (12,388 feet), Japan's highest mountain. Mount Fuji is a dormant volcano which last erupted in 1707. There are about 200 volcanoes in the Japanese Alps; many are active and lakes fill the craters of the dormant ones.

Southeast of Tokyo there is a long, narrow trench in the ocean floor almost six miles deep. The proximity of great ocean depths and towering heights on land produces stresses and strains in the earth's crust, and these cause earth tremors. Japan has about 1,500 earthquakes a year, but fortunately most of them do not cause much damage.

Mount Fuji, the highest peak in Japan (12,388 feet), is a sacred mountain to the Japanese. More than 50,000 pilgrims climb to the summit every year when the summer sun melts the snow crown. The long symmetrical slopes, which have made the mountain world-famous for its beauty, were formed by volcanic action and the summit contains the crater which is 500 feet deep.

Japanese rivers are short and flow swiftly down the mountainsides. The small lowlands, mostly at the heads of bays or in river valleys, are naturally important in so mountainous a country. The most important are along the northern shore of the Inland Sea; the largest is the 5,000 square-mile Kwanto Plain at the head of Tokyo Bay. Like the Koreans, Japanese farmers have terraced the hillsides to bring more land into cultivation. Most Japanese farms are very small.

Two thirds of Japan and most of Korea are forested, with broadleaf trees like oak and maple predominating. The forests provide not only timber but charcoal, which is burned as fuel in many Japanese homes. The forests also provide food—nuts, fruits and bamboo shoots.

The monsoon system of Asia influences the climate of Korea and Japan, especially in winter when cold, dry air flows out from Central Asia. In summer the air movement reverses and warm, humid air comes in from the Pacific. Japan's climate is also affected by offshore currents. Off the northwest coasts of Hokkaido and Honshu a cold current flows down from northern waters. In these areas, winters are bitterly cold with heavy snowfalls. A warm current off the southeast shores of Japan makes the climate there warmer than at the same latitudes on the Asian mainland. In southern Japan summers are warm and humid.

North of latitude 37°N. winters are too cold for growing crops. But farther south farmers can grow two crops a year, and in parts of Kyushu, three. In August and September typhoons frequently strike southern Japan, bringing torrential rain and winds of tremendous force, and damaging houses and crops.

Both Korea and Japan have irregular coastlines with many bays and inlets; and this has encouraged fishing on a large scale. No part of Japan is more than 75 miles from the sea.

Agriculture and Fisheries

In the Far East two out of every three people make their living from agriculture. The best farmlands are the alluvial plains and valleys, and they are mostly in the east, southeast and south of the region.

Most agriculture is subsistence farming. The farmers rarely have any modern machinery, but plow their fields with wooden plows drawn by bullocks or water buffaloes, plant and harvest their rice by hand and, except in China and Japan, do little to improve the fertility of their land. Life is precarious since most farmers depend on the rains brought by the monsoons. If the rains fail, the crops fail and famine follows.

Europeans and Americans brought plantation agriculture to the region. They cleared large areas of forest, especially in Ceylon and Malaysia, and planted crops like tea or rubber, usually specializing in one type of crop. They financed and directed the plantations; abundant labor was always available locally. Most of these plantations are now owned by Asians.

The main areas of plantation agriculture are in former British territories; for example, Ceylon

Top: fishing boats near Cochin on the Malabar Coast of southwest India. There are numerous fishing communities on India's coasts and efforts are being made to improve their primitive methods especially in transportation and refrigeration.

Below: a Javanese worker collecting tiny young fish in a paddy field. Fish is Southeast Asia's main protein source. If they live away from the coast, villagers usually raise fish in ponds, irrigation channels or rice fields.

Right: a farmer herding his sheep on the poor grazing lands of Iran. More than three-quarters of all Iranians make their living from farming, many from raising livestock. In summer nomads graze their flocks in mountain valleys and in winter move them down to warmer pastures. Below: Malaysian farmers drying pepper in the state of Sarawak. Their conical hats show that China once influenced this area.

(rubber and tea), India (tea) and Malaysia (palm oil and rubber). Indonesia, once Dutch colonial territory, produces coffee, sugar, tea, palm oil, rubber, tobacco, nutmeg and other spices.

Nearly all the world's rice is grown in Far Eastern countries. It is the main crop and basic food of the people. Asian farmers often rate the quality of their land by its capacity for producing rice. Good land will produce two crops a year, sometimes even three if there is enough rain or the land can be irrigated. Unfortunately rice takes nutrients out of the soil, so this kind of intensive cultivation tends to make the soil less and less fertile.

In the lowlands of China and Japan people farm intensively but carefully. Farmers never leave the fields fallow; they use crop rotations and manure their land. Yields per acre of rice are therefore high, but not in terms of yield per agricultural worker.

In India rice occupies a greater area than any other crop. Yields are lower than in China or Japan because farming methods are less efficient. There is no crop rotation and a lot of land is left fallow every year, sometimes serving as pasture for a few cattle, sheep and goats.

Only four countries—Burma, Thailand, Cambodia and South Vietnam—export rice. Their export surplus goes mostly to Ceylon, Hong Kong, Japan and Singapore.

Both India and China grow a lot of wheat. China grows nearly as much wheat as the United States but, like India, still has to import supplies from North America and Australia. China's production of corn, cotton and tobacco is second only to that of the United States. She also grows large crops of vegetables and is a leading tea producer.

Cotton is a cheap cloth for making the light clothing needed in the warm, humid climate of the Far East. China, India and Pakistan are all major producers. More than 75 per cent of the world's jute comes from the Ganges-Brahmaputra Delta in East Pakistan.

Draft animals are numerous in Far Eastern countries, but in some countries religious beliefs prohibit the eating of meat. To Hindus, for instance, the cow is a sacred symbol of the Earth Mother; the strict Buddhist will eat neither meat nor fish. Pigs and poultry, however, are kept by most families in China and the Philippines. In China, too, the raising of beef cattle is becoming more important. Large flocks of sheep and goats are kept in Afghanistan, Iran and Mongolia.

Japan's "meat" is fish. The average Japanese eats about 16 times as much fish as the average American. Japanese fleets fish in nearly all parts of the Pacific Ocean and their whaling ships go regularly to the Antarctic. China has a large fishing industry too; only Japan and Peru have larger fisheries.

The huge coniferous forests of northeast China and North Korea have not yet been fully exploited. Teak is exported from the forests of Burma and Thailand. Japan produces large quantities of wood pulp.

85

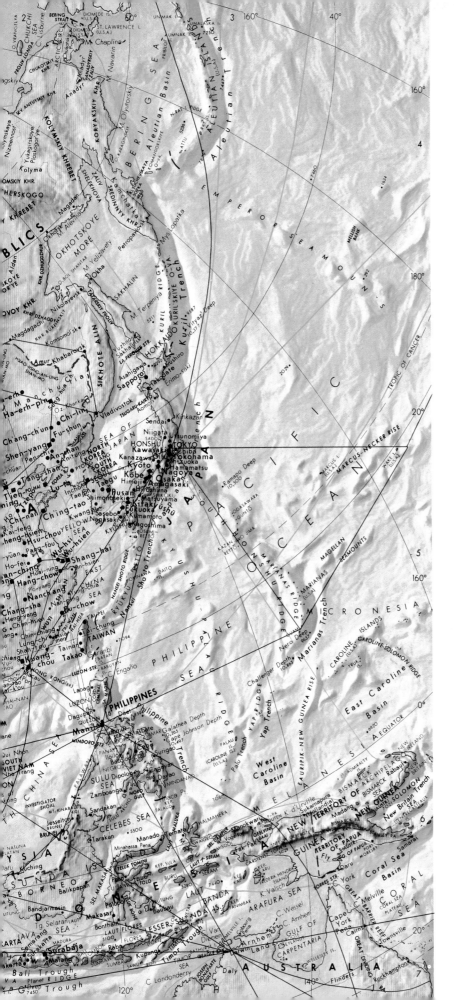

Eurasia

Projection: Lambert's Azimuthal Equal Area
Heights and depths in metres

Scale: 1: 41,900,000

Miles
0   200   400   600   800   1000   1200

Kilometres
0   200   400   600   800   1000   1200   1400   1600   1800

10,000 feet (3000 metres)
6000 feet (1800 metres)
3000 feet (900 metres)
1500 feet (450 metres)
1000 feet (300 metres)
500 feet (150 metres)
Sea level

Towns:

■ over 1,000,000
● over 500,000
• over 250,000
· under 250,000

〜〜 International boundaries
- - - Boundaries under dispute
〜 Major air routes
〜 Major sea routes

Mineral Resources and Industry

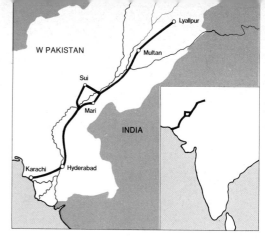

Map showing natural gas pipelines in West Pakistan. The gas, which is plentiful, is piped to Karachi (350 miles) and Multan (217 miles), and then 90 miles on to Lyallpur.

The mineral wealth of the Far East cannot be fully assessed because many countries have not carried out complete geological surveys. At present China, India, Japan, North Korea and North Vietnam seem the only countries with sufficient coal and iron to develop heavy industry.

China is tremendously rich in minerals. The annual output of her coal mines, which are mainly in the northeast, is already half that of the United States. There is abundant iron ore in Hopei, Shantung and other provinces; the deposits at Tayeh, near Hankow, are among the richest in the world. China is the world's chief producer of tungsten, and has large reserves of tin in Yunnan. She also has deposits of antimony, bauxite, copper, lead, manganese, mercury, silver and zinc.

India's coal fields are on the northeastern edge of the Deccan, about 200 miles northwest of Calcutta. The mines in the Damodar valley have thick seams that can be worked easily; and nearly all of India's coal comes from this field. There is also iron ore in the Deccan; the Singbhum deposits of high grade ore are among the world's largest. Limestone (used in steel production, and also for cement and fertilizers), chrome and manganese are also produced within 200 miles of Jamshedpur, the chief center of heavy industry.

Japan has some coal; her annual output, about 66 million metric tons, matches India's but is only one half of China's. About two million tons of iron ore are mined annually. These amounts are not enough to maintain Japan's heavy industry, and her position as the world's leading shipbuilding nation, so she has to import both coal (from the United States) and iron ore (from the United States and Australia). Japan has a wide range of other minerals including copper, lead, manganese, tungsten, asbestos and chrome.

Chromite, manganese, gold, some coal and iron ore are mined in the Philippines. North Korea has some coal and iron ore; South Korea, one of the world's largest deposits of tungsten. North Vietnam has the most valuable coal and iron ore deposits in Southeast Asia.

Part of a steel plant at Anshan (Liaoning province), China's largest steel center. China is the world's sixth largest iron and steel producer and continues to develop her heavy industry. Meanwhile consumer goods production has lagged.

Two thirds of the world's tin comes from Southeast Asia. Malaysia, Indonesia (the islands of Bangka, Belitung and Singkep) and Thailand are the chief producers.

Indonesia and Iran produce about six per cent of the world's crude petroleum and probably have 15 per cent of the world's petroleum reserves. The oil fields of Afghanistan, Burma, Japan, West Pakistan and China do not produce enough to meet local needs.

Hydroelectric power is being developed in many countries. In Japan, where the rivers are short and swift-flowing, with many waterfalls, there are more than 1,500 installations, supplying about half Japan's needs of electricity. Afghanistan, Pakistan, India, Ceylon and China have all set up hydroelectric projects. In some cases these are multipurpose, providing flood control and irrigation as well as power.

The industrial revolution only came to Asia a hundred years after it had reached North America, and even now development is hampered by the lack of good road and rail networks. So manufacturing is limited in most countries to supplying local needs.

Japan is the only country with what might be called a balanced industrial development. Sixty per cent of the Japanese work in non-agricultural jobs, compared with only 25 per cent in India and 20 per cent in China. But Japan relies largely on imported raw materials. The Japanese economy depends heavily on the export of manufactured goods to the United States and Europe. Japan is a major producer of radios, cameras and textiles and, with China and Hong Kong, has led Asia for a long time in the production of cheap consumer goods like bicycles, clothing and shoes.

Top: the Durgapur steel works, 100 miles northwest of Calcutta, India. Although the Deccan Plateau has good coal and iron deposits, India is short of steel. Production amounts to about 6,500,000 tons a year, one twentieth of the United States' annual steel output.

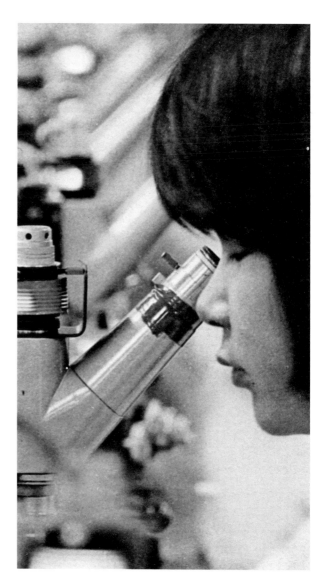

Woman worker at the Sony Corporation plant, Tokyo, which manufactures radio and tape-recording equipment of which Japan is a leading world producer. But it is in heavy industry that Japan is increasing her export trade most spectacularly.

Life in India and the Far East

Hindu pilgrims bathing in the Ganges River, India. They believe the river is sacred and its waters capable of curing disease. Some pilgrims bottle the water to send to relatives and friends in other parts of the world.

Almost two billion people, more than half the world's population, live in Asia, which covers more than one third of the earth's land surface. This continent has a higher population density than any other. Most people live in communities that hug the fertile alluvial land along the coasts and inland along river valleys. Hardly anyone lives in the mountains and deserts.

Plateaus, mountain ranges and deserts divide up Asia, so people have developed various different languages and cultures. There are several main racial groups but many people in the Far East are a mixture of races. Aetas, Ainu, Bengalis, Burmese, Japanese, Koreans, Malays, Maio, Pathans, Senois, Tamils, Thais and Uighurs are only some of the many different groups. Hundreds of separate languages and dialects have developed from the main language families. For example, the 499 million people in India speak 16 major languages. The people of Ceylon, China, Malaysia, Pakistan and the Philippines also have no common tongue. Another barrier to national unity in India is the caste system. Although the Government made caste discrimination illegal in the 1950's, it still prevails among the majority of the population.

In spite of race and language differences within a country, there may be certain common religious beliefs and customs. Roughly three quarters of the people of India are Hindus. Racial groups of different nations are linked by common religious beliefs too. Buddhism began in India 2,500 years ago. Today people follow this faith in Burma, Cambodia, Ceylon, China, Japan, Laos, Tibet, Thailand and Vietnam. Islam spread into the Far East from Arabia and now links people in Afghanistan, Iran, India, Indonesia, Malaysia, Pakistan and Mindanao (in the Philippines).

The Philippines is the only Christian country of the Far East; and, with Japan, the most westernized. Filipinos are Polynesians and speak a language related to those of Indonesia and Malaysia. In their relationships with Southeast Asia the Japanese, too, like to stress their Malay connections, but historically Japan has stronger associations with Korea and China.

China, in spite of certain differences between north and south, has a cultural unity from a civilization that persisted for over 4,000 years. Today Communism is the new link between the people of China, Mongolia, North Vietnam and North Korea—half the population of the Far East.

The biggest problem in both Communist and non-Communist Asia is rapid population increase, due as much to a falling death rate as an increased birth rate. The population goes up by about 80,000 a day. So each year there are millions more to feed and more and more people go hungry. India and Japan have started birth control programs and the Chinese Government has taken steps to curb population increase.

Scientists have been able to check some widespread diseases like malaria and bubonic plague by using DDT to get rid of carrier-mosquitos and fleas. Governments are trying to relieve hardship by importing food supplies and distributing them to famine-stricken areas. Diets consist mostly of cereal grains like wheat and rice and people eat little meat or fish, partly because of religious taboos and partly because meat protein is not readily available.

Illiteracy is another problem. Japan is the only wholly literate nation, since education has been free and compulsory from six to 15 for 100 years. But in India over half the men and over 80 per cent of the women cannot read or write. New schools and education centers are being built, but the question remains: Will building programs ever keep up with population growth?

The main street in Jaipur, capital of Rajasthan state, northern India. The picture shows (center right) the Palace of Winds, the former home of a maharajah, which contains many fine art treasures. Although many Indian cities have modern sections with large stores and office blocks, the older parts are crowded with slum dwellings, often without proper water supplies and sanitation.

Below: dancers celebrating a good harvest in Assam, northeast India. But harvests are poor if the monsoon rains fail. In India where most people are underfed, a good harvest can make all the difference between life and death.

Above: Buddhist monks at prayer in a Bangkok temple. They are a familiar sight in Thailand. More than 90 per cent of the population is Buddhist and there are more than 19,000 Buddhist temples. Every Buddhist male is expected to spend at least six months of his life in a monastery and to beg for alms.

Left: Temple of the Emerald Buddha (Wat Phra Keo), one of the most magnificent in the old city of Bangkok which has 300 Buddhist temples. Their gilded eaves, gaily tiled roofs, and porcelain-encrusted spires are in striking contrast to the stark new office blocks and factories.
Below: an agriculturalist, working under the United States' Point Four Program, demonstrates a new type of plowshare. Fitted to his wooden plow, the simple steel blade enables the farmer to cut deep furrows and so increase his crop yields.

Asians have a low standard of living compared with Europeans and North Americans. Most of the rural population are subsistence farmers, growing just enough to feed their families. Farmers use primitive tools and struggle to make a living, hampered by crop diseases and bad weather.

One in three Asians lives in a town or city. There are many cities with populations of more than a million; and more than five million people live in Calcutta, Shanghai, Peking and Tokyo. The majority of these large cities are ports and some stretch inland along river banks. Some cities like Tokyo and Manila have modern development areas. But even so, wages are usually low since there is abundant supply of labor.

Japan is the only country in the Far East with a really high standard of living. In the nineteenth century she adopted Western industrial methods and in less than a hundred years has managed to bridge the huge gulf between the feudalism of old Japan and ways of life in the Western world. The change has been spectacularly quick. Japan is now a leader in iron and steel, shipbuilding, electronics and other industries. Japanese railroads have crack expresses that any country might envy. Three of every 100 Japanese has his own car—a higher percentage than in any other Asian country. A network of express highways is under construc-

Like its counterpart in Moscow, Peking's Red Square is a setting for carefully organized parades and demonstrations. Although it is the capital of China, Peking is not China's largest city. Shanghai, where more than 10 million people live, is the largest.

Hong Kong (the name means "fragrant harbor") is a British colony consisting of numerous small islands at the mouth of the Canton River, southeast China, and a foothold (Kowloon) on the mainland. Its population (about 3½ million) includes refugees from Communist China.

tion and the main islands are being linked by double-deck undersea highway tunnels. Nationalist China is another success story. Due to land reform programs, almost all of Formosa's 600,000 farmers own their own land; and with a growth rate second only to Japan's the island has become prosperous in the years since 1949, when the Nationalists were driven from the mainland.

Change in traditional ways of life in other Far Eastern countries is accompanying agricultural and industrial revolutions. The Chinese call this simultaneous development "advancing on two feet". Developments in China have been the most far-reaching. For centuries China was a backward agricultural country, and hunger and disease were rampant. Now the government is gradually carrying out reforms. The family unit is weakening. The government organizes "communes" where between 20,000 and 70,000 people live. A typical commune usually includes several small villages and a few towns. It is an administrative unit that integrates farming with all the affairs of the community. Communes pay particular attention to reforestation, water conservation and road building. Everything is shared: houses, nurseries, dining rooms, laundries; and the commune provides schools, clinics, technical training centers and homes for old people. Chinese women go out to work in the factories or

fields. Many of them no longer do their own housework; cleaners from the "personnel" service department clean their homes.

As in China, the majority of India's population depends on agriculture; 80 per cent live in more than half a million villages. The Indian Government is experimenting in community cooperation to try and raise living standards in rural areas. The country has been divided into areas of land, each including about 100 villages. Trained workers instruct villagers in modern farming methods and show them how to improve their health and modernize domestic industries. The government also provides financial grants for projects like road building, irrigation and cooperative marketing.

Other parts of non-Communist Asia are also developing agriculture and educating their people. In the Philippines a joint economic assistance program with the United States is helping thousands of farmers.

Many Far Eastern countries have only become independent since the end of World War II. The war caused a lot of hardship, and political and social upheavals have made progress in agriculture and industry difficult. But the Far East is gradually advancing with the help of outside assistance from the United States, the Soviet Union and the countries of Western Europe.

India, the Far East and the World

A Japanese shipyard. For more than ten years Japan has been the world's leading shipbuilding nation. She now builds more oil tankers in a year than Britain, Sweden and West Germany together. Japan is Asia's most highly industrialized country. Electrical and electronic equipment and other similar types of light industry are becoming increasingly important.

The vast size and population of India and the Far East make the bitter struggle for a better life of particular concern to countries all over the world. Asia's foreign exchange reserves are much lower and its trade deficits three times higher than twenty years ago. Population increases five times as fast as food production; food output is actually dropping in India, Pakistan, South Korea, and Nepal.

In these circumstances it is not surprising that countries once ruled by European nations maintain close relationships with Europe. India, Pakistan, Ceylon, Malaysia and Singapore are members of the British Commonwealth. All the non-Communist Asian countries have joined Australia, Britain, Canada, New Zealand, and the United States in the Colombo Plan. The non-Asian countries give capital and technical training and equipment to the underdeveloped nations, in order to promote economic development and raise living standards. The largest schemes are major engineering works like dams and power stations. The United States has its own plan—the Point Four Program—to help the development of non-Communist countries. And the World Health Organization is helping many countries combat disease, another major problem aggravated by malnutrition.

After the Korean War, some Asian countries entered military alliances with the Western powers. In 1954 Australia, France, New Zealand, Pakistan, the Philippines, Thailand, Britain and the United States formed the Southeast Treaty Organization (S.E.A.T.O.), a mutual defense pact against Communist aggression.

Now Communist China has become a world power. In 1964 she exploded her first nuclear device; and she now gives financial and technical aid to several countries in Asia, the Middle East and Africa. Like the U.S.S.R., China bases eco-nomic development on a system of five-year plans. Although she has increased industrial and agricultural production, the people have to go without many things that West Europeans and North Americans think essential.

In spite of severe economic problems Asia is important in the world's trade. Most exports of the Far East are either agricultural or raw materials for industry. Pakistan, India and Southeast Asia provide most of the world's jute, natural rubber and tea; India and Ceylon are two of the world's largest tea producers. These regions also produce more than one third of the world's vegetable oils and fats, and two thirds of the tin. Imports are mainly machinery and manufactured goods. Former British territories still trade mostly with Britain and other Commonwealth countries; trade between Indonesia and the Netherlands has dramatically increased during the past few years; the Philippines still trades mainly with the United States.

Japan, the only country in Asia with a highly developed industrial economy, imports raw materials, mainly from the United States, and exports manufactures.

Three quarters of China's trade is with other Communist states, although her trade with non-Communist countries is increasing. China exports raw materials like tin and tungsten; and some light machinery. She imports wheat from Canada and Australia and oil and machinery from the U.S.S.R.

Providing their countries with stable economies is a big task for Asian governments. The population explosion, low living standards and illiteracy are only some of the problems. And nearly all of Asia is caught up in the struggle between Communism and Western democracy. This has actually led to war in two countries—Korea and Vietnam—and the division of each country into two political units.

Republic Day parade in New Delhi, the capital of India. The old city of Delhi containing the palace of the Mogul emperor Shah Jehan (1592-1966) and his great mosque, the Jama Masjid, stands on the west bank of the Jumna River. New Delhi, built as the capital in 1912, stands 5 miles to the southwest.

COUNTRIES OF THE FAR EAST

1 AFGHANISTAN
2 BHUTAN
3 BRUNEI
4 BURMA
5 CAMBODIA
6 CEYLON
7 CHINA (COMMUNIST)
8 CHINA (NATIONALIST)
9 INDIA

AFGHANISTAN*
Kingdom
S.W. Asia
Area: 254,000 sq. miles

Pop: 15,909,000. **Land use** %: mountainous 75; desert 25; cultivation limited to oases and few large irrigated valleys. **Occupations:** agriculture, pastoral (sheep), trading. **Industries:** silk, woollen and cotton cloth and carpet manufacture. **Capital:** Kabul (450,000).

BHUTAN
Kingdom (Protectorate of India)
Central Asia
Area: 18,000 sq. miles

Pop: 750,000. **Land use:** mountainous, lower slopes forested, limited primitive agriculture. **Occupations:** agriculture, animal husbandry and handicrafts. **Capital:** Thimphu.

BRUNEI
U.K.-protected Sultanate
E. Indies
Area: 2,000 sq. miles

Pop: 84,000. **Land use:** extensive forests, but plantation and subsistence farming. **Occupations:** plantation (rubber) and subsistence agriculture, forestry. **Industries:** petroleum, **Capital:** Brunei (53,000).

BURMA*
Republic
S.E. Asia
Area: 262,000 sq. miles

Pop: 25,246,000. **Land use** %: waste 53; forest and woodland 34; cultivated 13. **Occupations:** agriculture, industry, trade. **Industries:** processing raw materials, e.g. timber, rice, tobacco, minerals. **Capital:** Rangoon (1,530,000).

CAMBODIA*
Kingdom
S.E. Asia
Area: 70,000 sq. miles

Pop: 6,300,000. **Land use** %: forest 75; cultivated 25. **Occupations:** agriculture, fishing, forestry, mining. **Industries:** textile, handicraft. **Capital:** Phnom-Penh (600,000).

CEYLON* †
Constitutional Monarchy
Southern Asia
Area: 25,000 sq. miles

Pop: 11,500,000. **Land use** %: forest 54; waste 25; cultivated 21. **Occupations:** agriculture, trade and transport, professions, industry and mining, etc. **Industries:** processing agricultural products, china and pottery, vegetable oils, chemicals. **Capital:** Colombo (512,000).

CHINA (COMMUNIST)
Republic
E. Asia
Area: 3,700,000 sq. miles

Pop: 760,000,000. **Land use** %: waste 62; grassland 20; cultivated 9; forest 9. **Occupations:** agriculture, mining, industry, fishing. **Industries:** iron and steel, coal, textiles, petroleum. **Capital:** Peking (5,420,000).

CHINA (NATIONALIST)*
Republic
China Sea
Area: 14,000 sq. miles

Pop: 12,993,000. **Land use** %: forest 59; cultivated 24; waste 15; grassland 2. **Occupations:** agriculture, fishing. **Industries:** processing of agricultural products. **Captial:** Taipei (1,149,000).

INDIA* †
Republic
S. Asia
Area: 1,262,000 sq. miles

Pop: 498,860,000. **Land use** %: cultivated 46; waste 41; forest 13. **Occupations:** agriculture, industry, trade. **Industries:** coal, iron and steel, cement, paper, textiles. **Capital:** Delhi (2,712,000).

INDONESIA*
Republic
S.E. Asia
Area: 736,000 sq. miles

Pop: 110,000,000. **Land use** %: forest 63; waste 31; cultivated 6. **Occupations:** agriculture, mining, manufacturing. **Industries:** petroleum refining, rubber, foodstuffs, handicrafts. **Capital:** Djakarta (3,500,000).

IRAN (Persia)*
Kingdom
S.W. Asia
Area: 628,000 sq. miles

Pop: 25,781,000. **Land use** %: waste 72; forest 12; cultivated 10; grassland 6. **Occupations:** subsistence agriculture, pastoral. **Industries:** petroleum refining, textiles, crafts. **Capital:** Tehran (2,803,000).

JAPAN*
Constitutional Monarchy
Islands, E. Asia
Area: 143,000 sq. miles

Pop: 99,720,000. **Land use** %: forest 60; waste 17; cultivated 15; grassland 8. **Occupations:** agriculture, forestry, manufacturing, commerce, public services. **Industries:** iron and steel, heavy engineering, shipbuilding, cement, chemicals, textiles, rubber, paper, oil refining etc. **Capital:** Tokyo (13,788,000).

KOREA (NORTH)
Republic
E. Asia
Area: 47,000 sq. miles

Pop: 12,100,000. **Land use:** mountainous, with fertile plains and valleys. **Occupations:** agriculture, fishing, industry, mining. **Industries:** iron and steel, machinery, chemicals, textiles, handicrafts. **Capital:** Pyongyang (286,000).

KOREA (SOUTH)
Republic
E. Asia
Area: 38,000 sq. miles

Pop: 29,194,000. **Land use:** mountain, forest and fertile plains. **Occupations:** agriculture, fishing, mining. **Industries:** textiles, processing agricultural products. **Capital:** Seoul (3,471,000).

10 INDONESIA
11 IRAN (PERSIA)
12 JAPAN
13 KOREA (NORTH)
14 KOREA (SOUTH)
15 LAOS
16 MALAYSIA
17 MALDIVE ISLANDS
18 MONGOLIA

19 NEPAL
20 PAKISTAN
21 PHILIPPINES
22 SIKKIM
23 SINGAPORE
24 THAILAND (SIAM)
25 VIETNAM (NORTH)
26 VIETNAM (SOUTH)

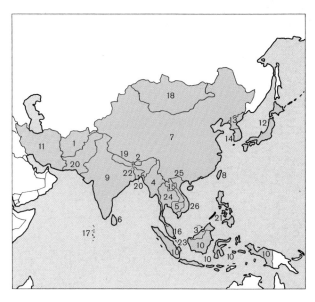

LAOS*
Kingdom
S.E. Asia
Area: 91,000 sq. miles

Pop: 3,000,000. **Land use %:** waste 32; forest and woodland 60; meadow and pasture 4; arable and orchard 4. **Occupations:** agriculture, mining, forestry. **Industries:** processing agricultural products, textiles, cement. **Capital:** Vientiane (125,000).

MALAYSIA* †
Federation
S.E. Asia
Area: 128,000 sq. miles

Pop: 9,661,000. **Land use:** forest 74; cultivated 16; Waste 10 **Occupations:** agriculture, fishing, forestry, commerce, manufacturing. **Industries:** rubber, tobacco, cement, foodstuffs, petroleum, consumer goods. **Capital:** Kuala Lumpur (500,000).

MALDIVE ISLANDS* †
Sultanate
Indian Ocean
Area: 115 sq. miles

Pop: 97,000. **Land use:** intensively cultivated. **Occupations:** agriculture, fishing, trading. **Capital:** Malé (11,000).

MONGOLIA*
Republic
Central Asia
Area: 600,000 sq. miles

Pop: 1,104,000. **Land use %:** grassland 70; desert and tundra 22; forest 8. **Occupations:** nomadic herdsmen, mining. **Industries:** processing animal products, light engineering. **Capital:** Ulan Bator (195,000).

NEPAL*
Constitutional Monarchy
Central Asia
Area: 54,000 sq. miles

Pop: 10,294,000. **Land use:** mostly waste, cultivation in deep valleys and lowlands. **Occupations:** agriculture, forestry, mining. **Capital:** Katmandu (225,000).

PAKISTAN* †
Republic
S. Asia
Area: 366,000 sq. miles

Pop: 105,044,000. **Land use %:** waste 76; cultivated 21; forest 3. **Occupations:** agriculture. **Industries:** textiles, processing agricultural products, consumer goods. **Capital:** Rawalpindi (340,000). **Capital designate:** Islamabad.

PHILIPPINES*
Republic
E. Asian Islands
Area: 116,000 sq. miles

Pop: 33,477,000. **Land use %:** forest 53; cultivated 27; waste 17; grassland 3. **Occupations:** agriculture, forestry, fishing, mining, manufacturing. **Capital:** Manila (2,256,000); **Capital designate:** Quezon City.

SIKKIM
Kingdom (Indian Protectorate)
Central Asia
Area: 3,000 sq. miles

Pop: 162,000. **Land use:** mainly waste. **Occupations:** primitive agriculture in deep valleys, forestry. **Industries:** textiles. **Capital:** Gangtok (12,000).

SINGAPORE* †
Republic
S.E. Asia,
Area: 225 sq. miles.

Pop: 2,000,000. **Occupations:** shipping, commerce. **Industries:** ship building, tin smelting, light industry. **Capital:** Singapore.

THAILAND (SIAM)*
Kingdom
S.E. Asia
Area: 198,000 sq. miles

Pop: 31,800,000. **Land use %:** forest 64; waste 27; cultivated 9. **Occupations:** agriculture (rice), forestry, fishing, commerce, mining. **Industries:** cement, textiles, handicrafts, processing agricultural products, foodstuffs. **Capital:** Bangkok (1,800,000).

VIETNAM (NORTH)
Republic
S.E. Asia
Area: 66,000 sq. miles

Pop: 19,000,000. **Land use %:** mountainous 80; cultivated 20. **Occupations:** agriculture (rice), fishing, coal mining. **Industries:** timber, cement, textiles, chemicals. **Capital:** Hanoi (645,000).

VIETNAM (SOUTH)
Republic
S.E. Asia
Area: 66,000 sq. miles

Pop: 16,543,000. **Land use:** mountainous forest and grasslands over 5000 feet; intensive cultivation in river valleys. **Occupations:** agriculture (rice); fishing, mining. **Industries:** rubber, timber, chemicals, foodstuffs. **Capital:** Saigon (2,000,000 with Cholon).

* Member of the United Nations
† Member of the British Commonwealth

NORTH AMERICA

North America, a region of incredible contrasts, is the third largest continent after Asia and Africa. The United States alone has an area of 3½ million square miles, and Canada is even larger. Every kind of natural challenge, from icy waste and mountain barrier to burning desert and steaming swamp, faced the pioneers and frontiersmen who built these two great and growing nations.

Left above: rocky coast of Maine near Portland. This state's irregular coastline with its many peninsulas, finger-like inlets and bays, measures more than 2,500 miles. Because of its beautiful coast, mountains and forests, Maine is a popular vacation state.

Right above: fishermen collecting their catch in the Bay of Fundy. This bay, which separates Nova Scotia from New Brunswick and Maine, has the world's greatest tides, the range between high and low tide often exceeding 40 feet. The great tidal force sweeps the fish into the nets to be collected when the tide ebbs.

Left: the dark silhouette of a fishing shed, a tranquil sea and a pale orange sunset at Peggy's Cove, Nova Scotia. This Canadian province is probably better known for its Annapolis apple orchards than for its coal and fishing industries.

North Atlantic Seaboard

The six small New England states and the Canadian Atlantic provinces lie along the northeast coast of North America. A region of thin, poor soils and harsh climate, this was one of the first in the New World to be settled by Europeans. In the early days of settlement people stayed close to the sea; fishing, whaling, boat building; and maritime industries have flourished here ever since.

At first mountains were an impenetrable barrier between the coastal colonies and the interior. The great Appalachians stretch north from Alabama about 1,400 miles to the Gaspé Peninsula at the mouth of the St. Lawrence River and then reappear in Newfoundland. From the rocky, indented island-strewn coasts of the Canadian Atlantic provinces, the land rises to mountain masses overlooking the Gulf of St. Lawrence. The Shickshock Mountains reach over 4,000 feet. But there are some lowland plains in north Nova Scotia, east New Brunswick and on Prince Edward Island. During the Ice Age glaciers either stripped the rock bare or deposited sand and gravel in valleys of the Canadian provinces. Thick forest covers this sandy soil region.

But there is good farmland in the fertile lowlands bordering the St. Lawrence. This ribbon of intensive agriculture, 80 miles across at its widest, suffers from severe winters with temperatures well below freezing. But summers are long and warm enough for farmers to grow oats, hay and root crops and keep livestock like cattle and pigs. Long, straggling villages lie close to the river, and narrow fields stretch back to the forest edge. Montreal, one of Canada's important industrial towns and largest ports, stands in these lowlands. Ocean ships can navigate the St. Lawrence River, one of North America's great water highways, 1,000 miles upstream as far as Montreal. But in winter the St. Lawrence freezes over for four or five months.

Canso Causeway sweeps across the narrow stretch of sea between Cape Breton Island and mainland Nova Scotia. Opened in 1955, the causeway carries a road and railroad— vital land transport links for Cape Breton's coal, iron ore and other industries.

The three isolated maritime provinces of Canada and the island of Newfoundland are relatively undeveloped, but they are rich in natural resources. Bell Island off the northern coasts of Newfoundland has large iron ore deposits. Newfoundland also has copper, lead and zinc; New Brunswick has coal, gypsum and other minerals; and near Sydney on Cape Breton Island are some of the largest coal deposits in Canada. Besides the mineral resources both for industrial raw materials and power, the provinces have tremendous hydroelectric power potential.

Halifax, Nova Scotia, is the only leading Canadian port that stays ice-free all winter. Most towns of the Atlantic provinces are near the coast and two thirds of the people live in country districts poorly served by road and rail transport. Farmers depend on a short growing season from May to October, and thin soils limit agriculture scope. Yet the Atlantic provinces are well known for their apples, from the orchards of the Annapolis Valley, Nova Scotia, and their seed potatoes, grown in New Brunswick and Prince Edward Island.

In the six New England States, Maine, New Hampshire, Vermont, Massachusetts, Connecticut and Rhode Island, the landscape is like the Canadian Atlantic provinces: rocky coasts, inland forests and minimal good farmland. The great bays like Boston Harbor are ideal for shipping, and most American ships operate from Atlantic harbors. The United States' first manufacturing centers were set up along New England's short, swift-flowing rivers, using water power to drive machinery. Early emphasis on manufacturing was the basis of New England's prosperity. Textile mills, tanneries, foundries and boot and shoe factories grew up and prospered with the opening up of the interior. Factories drew a lot of their raw materials, like wool and hide, from the surrounding countryside. But the development of large-scale agriculture in the west made some farm products cheaper to produce there and the New England farmers could not meet the competition. Now farmers specialize in dairying and crops like cranberries and sweet corn for canning; and people vacation in the hills and forests.

The New England states have no coal or iron ore and few other minerals. So when coal became the primary power source many factories moved to the southwest, nearer the Appalachian coal field; but southern New England is still a major manufacturing and commercial center, and New England has twelve times as many large towns as the Canadian Atlantic provinces.

Atlantic Ocean

Projection: Mercator
Heights and depths in metres

Scale: 1:71,200,000 equatorial scale

Miles
0   500   1000   1500   2000

0   500   1000   1500   2000   2500   3000
Kilometres

Ice caps

10,000 feet
(3000 metres)
6000 feet
(1800 metres)
3000 feet
(900 metres)

1500 feet
(450 metres)
1000 feet
(300 metres)
500 feet
(150 metres)

Sea level

International
boundaries
Major
air routes
Major
sea routes

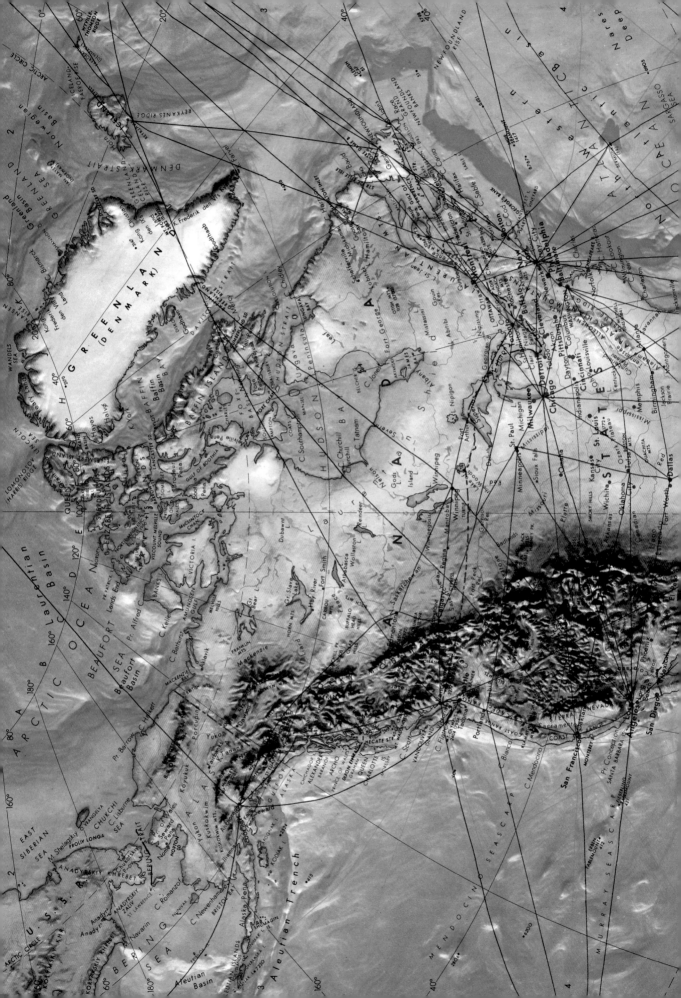

North America

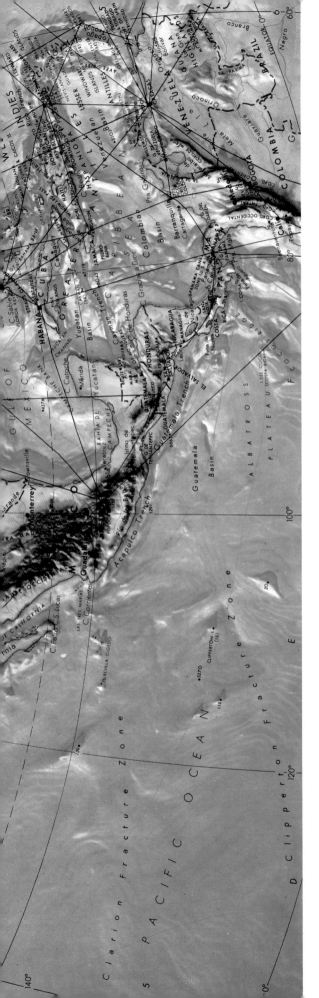

Projection: Lambert's Equal Area
Heights and depths in metres

Scale: 1:32,100,000

Miles

| 0 | 200 | 400 | 600 | 800 |

Kilometres

| 0 | 200 | 400 | 600 | 800 | 1000 | 1200 | 1400 |

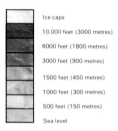

Ice caps

10,000 feet (3000 metres)

6000 feet (1800 metres)

3000 feet (900 metres)

1500 feet (450 metres)

1000 feet (300 metres)

500 feet (150 metres)

Sea level

Towns:

■ over 1,000,000

● over 500,000

● over 250,000

• under 250,000

International boundaries

Major air routes

Major sea routes

Top: peaceful scene in Central Park, New York City. This park is more than twice the size of the principality of Monaco. Above: this church is at Farmington, a small town southwest of Hartford, Connecticut. Settled in 1640, Farmington has many fine old buildings. Right: Chicago is the focal point of 20 major railroads. Its O'Hare Airport is the world's busiest. It is also a leading port, and a manufacturing center.

Northeast Industrial States

Above: the Appalachian Mountains. They are a 1,400-mile long system of parallel ranges stretching from the Gaspé Peninsula in Quebec, Canada, to central Alabama. They are highest in North Carolina, where Mount Mitchell reaches 6,684 feet.

Left: blast furnaces at Pittsburgh, Pennsylvania. This city, standing where the Allegheny and Monongahela Rivers meet to form the Ohio River, has some of America's largest steel plants and produces more steel than any other city in the world, using coal from the Appalachian coal field and iron ore from the Great Lakes ports.

The industrial northeast stretches west from New England as far as Chicago, to Montreal in the north and to Baltimore in the south. About two fifths of the people of the United States and a quarter of the Canadians live in this region. But it is not continuously built up like the industrial areas of Northwest Europe.

The coastal plain on the eastern United States starts at Cape Cod and widens out as it spreads south. New York City, the commercial and financial capital of North America, stands at the junction of rocky New England and the sandy coastal lowlands. Manhattan is built on a rocky island at the mouth of the Hudson River while Long Island is sandy. New York, the world's largest port, is built around eight large bays and four straits, giving a fine natural harbor. This giant metropolis is a large and concentrated consumer market—New Yorkers eat about one twelfth of the food consumed in the United States.

Baltimore, Philadelphia and many other large cities are within 200 miles of New York. Farms on the coastal plain supply the needs of this large urban market.

The Appalachian Mountains lie inland from the coastal plain. From east to west these mountains form four regions. Just east of the Blue Ridge, forests cover the undulating upland of the Piedmont. Streams flow easily over its surface but tumble at the Fall Line in a succession of rapids. Towns like Trenton on the Delaware grew at this point all along the edge of the Piedmont. The Blue Ridge stretches for 600 miles from the Schuylkill River to north Georgia. It is wooded too and mostly over 4,000 feet high. West of the Blue Ridge, the Ridge and Valley section extends all the way from the St. Lawrence lowlands into Alabama. Narrow, flat-topped, wooded ridges alternate with fertile valleys. The rivers swing from one side of the valleys to the other and sometimes cut through the ridges.

West of the Ridge and Valley section the rugged Appalachian Plateau rises up to 2–3,000 feet. Its rocks are almost horizontal and the headstreams of the Ohio score the plateau in the north. The Appalachian coal field lies under the Plateau. The rivers made deep cuts, exposing the four-feet thick, horizontal coal seams. Conditions for mechanical cutting and loading are ideal and output per miner is the highest in the world.

Many of these coal mining valleys converge on

Aerial view of Lower Manhattan Island showing New Jersey and the Hudson River (left) and the East River (right). A system of bridges and tunnels connects the island with New York City's four other boroughs. Manhattan Island, about 13 miles long and two miles wide, is the business, financial and cultural heart of the city.

Pittsburgh. Drawing on resources and coal from the surrounding countryside, Pittsburgh makes pig iron and glass; and produces more steel than any other city in the world.

The Appalachian barrier has been crossed at great expense by railroads and the Pennsylvania Turnpike. The easiest way, although not the most direct, through the Appalachians from the east coast to the interior was along the Hudson and Mohawk valleys. Manufacturing towns dotted along this busy route make all kinds of goods, from electric generators to dominos.

The Great Lakes (Ontario, Erie, Huron, Michigan and Superior) form the world's largest group of inland lakes. During the Ice Age glaciers covered North America as far south as the Missouri and Ohio Rivers. The retreating ice sheets left behind low morainic ridges which dammed the melting water. The water spread out behind these ridges fingering into the Canadian Shield to the north and forming the Great Lakes.

Ocean-going ships can sail right up to the Great Lakes by way of the St. Lawrence Seaway. The Lakes are also linked by canal with the Ohio and Mississippi Rivers to the south. Many of the cities around the shores owe much of their importance to Great Lakes trade. Detroit, on the Detroit River between Lake Huron and Lake Erie, is one of the world's most important manufacturing cities. It is a gateway between eastern and western ports on the Lakes. But for four to five months in winter the Lakes are frozen over and closed to traffic.

Another view of Lower Manhattan looking south from the Empire State Building, the highest (1,472 feet over all) of New York's many skyscrapers. Fifth Avenue (center), stretches down to Washington Square, the meeting point of the old city to the south and the newer checker-board pattern of streets and avenues.

Washington, D.C., the federal capital of the United States, occupies a site on the northwest bank of the Potomac River selected by George Washington himself. The city, the first to be planned as a national capital, was the work of French engineer, Major Pierre L'Enfant, whose design produced one of the most beautiful cities in the world. Its many notable buildings and monuments include the White House, the official residence of the President. First occupied in 1800, it was burned down by the British in 1814 and had to be rebuilt. The Washington Monument (extreme left) stands in a park by the Tidal Basin. This simple obelisk, faced with marble from Massachusetts and Maryland, rises to just over 555 feet. An elevator inside the monument takes sightseers to the 500-foot level. The Capitol (left) stands on Capitol Hill, 88 feet high. The north wing contains the Senate Chamber; the House of Representatives meets in the south wing. The great dome, nearly 300 feet high, is topped by Crawford's bronze Statue of Freedom.

A sandy, alluvial coastal plain lies east and south of the Appalachian Mountains. Plains stretch west from the Appalachians as far as the Rocky Mountains and north to the Canadian Shield. The Mississippi (one of the longest rivers in the world) and its tributaries drain these huge plains in the center of the continent.

East of the Appalachians, from Maryland to South Carolina, the coast plain is sandy and infertile with a pine forest cover. The Florida Peninsula is made of limestone. The Mississippi River is building huge alluvial plains in its lower valley and a great delta out into the Gulf of Mexico. Below St. Louis the Mississippi meanders slowly to the sea falling less than six inches per mile. After long periods of rain it floods but the river authorities are trying to avert this by building dikes and dredging the river bed deeper. Since 1933 the Tennessee Valley Authority has built dams to control the flood waters of the Tennessee River and these lessen the destruction caused by the flooding lower Mississippi. The lower Mississippi valley and the rest of the south have a very warm, humid climate with usually more than 200 frost-free days a year.

The plains are in the central belt of the continent. From the Arctic islands to the subtropical coast of the Gulf of Mexico there is no real barrier to the movement of winds (which may be bitterly cold from the north or very hot from the south). The plains are not all low. Cincinnati stands 600 feet above sea level and Edmonton, Alberta, 2,200 feet.

There are several upland areas in the interior plains of the United States. The rugged hill country of Kentucky and Tennessee, at its highest 1,400 feet, lies west of the Appalachian Plateau. Here are two basins: the Blue Grass Basin of Kentucky, famous for its racehorses, and the Nashville Basin of Tennessee. The Ozark Plateau and the Ouachita Mountains of Missouri and Arkansas reach over 1,000 feet and are the same age as the Appalachians.

During the Ice Age the ice sheet wore away the land north of the Great Lakes but to the south, as far as the Missouri and Ohio Rivers, the ice sheets deposited debris, filling in hollows until a smooth surface was formed. Morainic ridges dam the Great Lakes. Glacial deposits south of the Lakes provide some of the best farm land in the world; the Midwest includes sections of the Dairying, Spring Wheat and Corn Belts. Winds picking up the very fine material scattered it over Kansas and Nebraska.

The ice sheets missed a small area in southwest Wisconsin which is free of glacial deposits. Underneath the glacial material the structure of the plains is like a huge basin filled with deposits from surrounding ancient mountain masses. This process has been going on for hundreds of millions of years.

The Great Plains form the drier, higher western part of the interior plains. The north and western parts of the Spring Wheat Belt extend into the Great Plains, but with the exploitation of oil and natural gas in the region the economy is no longer solely dependent on agriculture. Farther south, broad terracelike plateaus border the Yellowstone River and its tributaries. The isolated Black Hills in South Dakota were formed the same time as the Rocky Mountains.

In the interior of any continental mass there are great temperature differences between summer and winter. In summer maximum temperatures rise above 90°F. and seldom drop below 65°F. at night. In winter it snows and temperatures may go down to −30°F. In the central plains rain comes mainly in summer and the farther west you go the drier it becomes. The weather may stay the same for long periods and when changes come they are sudden, often violent. Heavy thunderstorms, hailstorms or tornadoes alternate with dry periods. There is no gradual merging of the seasons—they are sharply defined.

Grassland once covered the whole of the interior plains west of Ohio, and sheep and cattle still graze the grasses of the Great Plains in the west. In the east where there is most rain, the grasses could grow up to 10 feet high, but most of the ground has been ploughed up and planted with corn and other cereal crops.

West of 100°W the Great Plains have a lower rainfall and so much shorter grasses grow, becoming patchy in the dryer parts. Trees only grow in river valleys or on isolated mountains like the Black Hills.

Wheat fields in Illinois. This state has some of the world's
richest soil; nine out of every ten acres are farmland. Illinois
also has coal and petroleum deposits. More than half the state's
population of over 10 million live in the Chicago area.

The United States is rich in scenic beauty and
natural wonders. There is endless variety in its
landscapes and some are unique. They include
the majestic Rocky Mountains (top left), which
run through western North America from northern
Alaska to northern New Mexico. Several national
parks, including the famous Yellowstone National
Park, come within this range. A contrast is
provided by the idyllic Shenandoah Valley (above)
between the Blue Ridge and Allegheny Mountains. The Shenandoah River, about 55 miles
long, flows from Virginia across the northeast
corner of West Virginia to join the Potomac at
Harper's Ferry. Yet another contrast is found on
the San Juan River, whose fantastic bends
(right) occur as it flows through southeast Utah
to join the Colorado River near Rainbow Bridge
National Monument.

From the Rockies to the Pacific

Irrigation in west United States. Note the large number of irrigated farms in the Central Valley (Sacramento and San Joaquin Rivers) of California.

Each dot represents 200 irrigated farms

From the western edge of the Great Plains the land begins to rise steeply into a system of mountain ranges towering over 10,000 feet. These are young fold mountains like the Alps, crumpled, fractured and pushed up by earth movements.

The Rockies, the easternmost chain of the Pacific highlands, stretch almost without interruption from Alaska to Mexico. These bold rugged mountains are often snow-capped and their lower slopes are covered with forests. There are two breaches in the Rockies; in the extreme north of Canada below Brook's Range, and the Wyoming Basin in the United States.

A tract of plateau and basin country lies between the Rockies and the Pacific coast ranges. The plateaus sometimes descend from the Rockies like a series of steps as far down as Death Valley, California, 282 feet below sea level. The Great Basin centered on Nevada is a desert region circled by mountains which block the flow of most of the rivers. Only streams in the extreme north and south drain down to the sea; the rest dry up or flow into lakes. The water in lakes like the Great Salt Lake is extremely salty, much more than the ocean. The Colorado Plateau lies south of the Great Basin. The Colorado River and its tributaries have cut into the plateau's horizontal rocks to form canyons like the 5,000 foot-deep Grand Canyon. The British Columbia Plateau is a great area of basalt lava which welled up through volcanic fissures and spread out.

The Pacific coast mountains are really two chains separated by a trough. The eastern chain runs south through the Cascades and Sierra Nevada; and the western through the coast ranges of Washington, Oregon and California. The Strait of Georgia, the Willamette Valley and the Central Valley of California make up the central trough.

The fertile Central Valley is 400 miles long and 50 miles wide. In some places the land has to be drained and in others, because of the summer

Salt Lake City, state capital of Utah, lies in the Salt Lake Valley near the Jordan River at the foot of the Wasatch Range. It was founded by the Mormons under Brigham Young over 100 years ago. The city serves a rich agricultural and mining area.

Hollywood Bowl, a large open-air theater famous for its concerts, lies in the heart of Hollywood, California, the most highly-publicized movie, television and radio center in the world. Hollywood, a district of Los Angeles, produces 90 per cent of all films made in the United States. In 1870 the district was farmland but now Hollywood has a population of more than 200,000, mainly living in apartments. More than 6 million people live in the Los Angeles urban area, a major American industrial center. Its harbor on San Pedro Bay is the largest man-made harbor in the world.

drought, irrigated. Farmers grow sub-tropical fruit like oranges, apricots, peaches, dates and figs as well as vegetables. Cotton is an important crop too. A large market for Central Valley farmers is San Francisco. This city, one of the great ports of North America, stands at the head of a promontory overlooking a large bay. It has a warm, humid climate and since it is exposed to the sea is often windy or fogbound.

South of the Central Valley the coast ranges rise almost straight out of the sea, but there is a lowland area around Los Angeles. A hydroelectric power station below the Hoover Dam on the Colorado River sends electricity to southern California and the reservoir provides water for irrigation in the same area. Although it is dry, the Los Angeles lowland has a good climate for agriculture and farmers can harvest several crops a year.

North from California forest-covered mountains border the ocean and the country is cool and moist. Giant redwoods and other tall trees flourish here. Mild weather is an asset to the Seattle shipbuilding industry since it is rarely too hot or too cold for the men to work outside.

More than 1,000 miles separate the eastern side of the Pacific highlands—the Great Continental Divide—from the Pacific coast. People once thought them impassable, but with the discovery of gold in

California and the 1849 gold rush thousands of prospectors crossed the Rockies. Other minerals like silver, lead, zinc and copper were sometimes found with the gold. Often as soon as the miners worked out the veins they deserted the towns.

The Rockies also divide up climate. West of the Rockies air masses coming in from the sea influence the climate and most rain comes in winter. To the east more than half the annual rainfall comes in summer since warm, moist air from the Gulf of Mexico affects this region.

Orange groves in California. The irrigation channels are fed by the melting snows on the San Bernardino Mountains in the background. Mount San Gorgonio (11,486 feet) is the highest peak.

The North

The Rocky Mountains system extends north along the Pacific coast into Alaska. Western Canada's coastline is like the fiord coast of Norway. Long, narrow inlets and creeks reach back into the mountains and innumerable islands scatter coastal waters. In Alaska, farmers grow apples and potatoes on the narrow coastal plain along sheltered fiords. The weather is cool and moist: Winter temperatures average 32°F., summer 60°F. and rain falls almost every day.

The interior plains, wedged between the Rockies and the Canadian Shield, extend north through Canada to the Arctic Ocean. The Canadian Shield covers more than half of Canada. The Shield, made of ancient crystalline rocks (granite, quartzite and gneiss) is the oldest part of the continent. It protrudes into the United States south of Lake Superior and in the Adirondack Mountains east of Lake Ontario. Broken up by countless hollows and hills, the Shield is usually about 1,000 feet above sea level. The region has numerous lakes and fast-flowing streams which often form rapids or waterfalls.

Ice sheets buried the whole of this region during the Ice Age. As we have already seen, morainic ridges dammed in the Great Lakes as the ice melted. But there were other large lakes too. Northwest of Lake Superior, Lakes Winnipeg, Winnipegosis and Manitoba are the remnants of a huge body of water.

Long, cold winters dominate this northern part of North America. Temperatures everywhere fall well below freezing point (32°F.) and more than

Top: a forest of red pine near Lake Erie. Trees like this provide useful timber for construction work. Erie is the fourth largest of the Great Lakes.
Below: an outpost in north Quebec. This is the oldest, largest and predominantly French-speaking province of Canada. Its capital is the city of Quebec. Its northern areas border Hudson Bay and Hudson Strait. Nearly half the province is forested, but it also produces most of Canada's asbestos and has important mines.

Canada's Mackenzie delta on the Arctic Ocean is tundra country. The soil is permanently frozen to a depth of many feet. In the short summer only the topsoil thaws, permitting the growth of lichens (pasture for caribou), small plants and occasional stunted willow. The underlying permafrost prevents trees from putting down deep roots, for support in the winter blizzards.

two thirds of Canada has temperatures of 0°F. in January. The frost period can last for more than six months; water mains and sewers are dug at least 7 feet below ground to stop them cracking in winter. Only British Columbia has January temperatures above freezing point. Summers are usually cool and short in the far north. The subsoil is permanently frozen and water lies on the ground in stagnant pools. These waterlogged areas, called muskegs, are mosquito breeding grounds in summer.

South of the tundra in northern Canada a broad belt of coniferous forest covers almost half the country extending south in places almost to the Canada-United States border and right across the continent from Yukon to Labrador. At the southern margins of the forest the timber industry and hydro-electricity have developed. As rivers cross the edge of the Shield they form waterfalls which power the generators. Canadian forests provide more than one third of the world's supply of wood pulp for newsprint.

The Canadian Shield has great mineral reserves too. The high grade iron ore deposits on the southern shores of Lake Superior, so important to the industries of the northeast, are now almost worked out. Only low grade ores are left. Recently the Canadians have discovered iron ore deposits in the forested wilderness of Labrador, 300 miles north of the St. Lawrence. This field probably has reserves of about 400 million tons. Mining only takes place in summer and railways link the mines with the coast. On Baffin Island prospectors have found 180 million tons of ore with an iron content of 69 per cent —the highest in the world. The Shield also produces a large part of the world's supply of gold, silver, nickel, platinum, copper, lead, zinc, radium and uranium.

Settlement in Canada crowds close to the United States' border. Most Canadian cities are south of latitude 50°N. Few people live north of this latitude, leaving an area larger than Europe almost empty. In the same latitudes in Europe there are 10 capital cities and dense concentrations of people. Canada, however, does not have a Gulf Stream like Northwest Europe. The climate and land are inhospitable and there are no road and rail networks.

Northern Canada is really too cold to grow many crops. Oats, rye and hay grow as far north as the Mackenzie lowlands or the Clay Belt around Hudson Bay in North Ontario; but poor soils, short growing seasons and isolation from large markets handicap northern farmers.

117

Agriculture and Fisheries

Pumpkins were first grown by North American Indians. Cultivation of this plant and corn, another Indian crop, was developed by the earliest settlers till today corn is one of the chief crops in the United States, the world leader in corn production.

Although in the past 30 years North American agriculture has gradually become more diversified, single crops still dominate large areas. North America grows all the crops she needs except for tropical products like coffee, cocoa, bananas, rubber and palm oil. Farm layouts in North America are different from those in western Europe. In the Midwest, government surveyors divided the land into square-mile sections of 640 acres. Quarter sections of 160 acres were made available as farms and early homesteads were based on this unit. In the west larger blocks were sold still based on 160 acres.

Corn is the United States' most important crop in aereage: she grows three times as much corn as wheat. The fertile Corn Belt runs through Iowa, Illinois, Indiana and Ohio. Farmers also keep pigs, cattle and poultry which eat most of the corn, converting it into meat.

Farms in Illinois, Indiana and Ohio grow wheat too. But corn usually needs more moisture than wheat; and between 20–40 inches of rain falls every year in the Corn Belt. Farmers do not usually grow corn where night temperatures in summer fall below 50°F. or where there are less than 150 frost-free days.

Canada and the United States produce almost one quarter of the world's wheat crop. Both countries have a large surplus, especially Canada which has only a small home market. The wheat lands of North America lie between latitudes 35°N. and 55°N., centered along longitude 100°W. In the Prairie Provinces of Canada and adjoining states of the United States, spring-sown wheat matures in about 100 days and needs 15–20 inches of rain. The Winter Wheat Belt includes Nebraska, Kansas and Oklahoma. The vast wheat farms, covering thousands of acres, are highly mechanized, and the Wheat Belts are sparsely populated.

You find truck farming and dairying near most towns. But immediately west, south and east of the

Top: an area of badly eroded land in the Mississippi Valley, one of the richest farming regions in the world. To prevent the valuable top soil from being washed into the river, tree planting is carried out to anchor the soil with the roots.
Bottom: eight years after the first photograph was taken. An identical view shows how the branching gullies have been completely re-clothed with sturdy loblolly pines. Self-seeded plants have begun to colonize the land in the foreground.

Automation on the Trelawney Farm owned by the Matthews family in Green County, Ohio. This view shows the beef cattle feeding factory where 300 head are fed in 45 minutes by pressing a button. Since the factory was built an annual production of 250 head of finished cattle has leapt to 900 head.

Great Lakes and north of the Corn Belt, astride the Canada-United States border, is a belt of mixed farming. Farmers grow hay and oats and keep dairy cattle for milk, butter and cheese.

Cotton and corn are the dominant farm crops in Texas, Louisiana, Arkansas, Mississippi, Tennessee, Alabama, Georgia and South Carolina. Cotton grows as far north as the 200 frost-free days limit and as far west as the 20-inch rainfall line. The Cotton Belt is not so dependent on one crop as it used to be. Farmers now grow cotton (still the most important cash crop) in rotation with fodder crops and soybeans for cattle. Farms in Texas are large and highly mechanized and farmers now harvest one third of the total cotton crop with machines.

Along the Gulf coast and southeast Atlantic coast, crops grow which need special soil and climate. Tobacco grows in a humid climate and nitrogenous soil. The main tobacco states are North Carolina, South Carolina, Virginia, Georgia, Kentucky and Tennessee. Florida produces oranges and grapefruit which only grow where there is no frost. Sugar cane grows on the rich alluvial soils of the Mississippi delta. Rice is grown in Texas, Louisiana and the lower Mississippi valley.

West of the main crop areas the climate is too dry for cultivation. Cattle and sheep graze on the huge expanses of plain or plateau. The greatest concentration of sheep is on the dry prairies of west Texas.

North American coniferous forests are consumed at an enormous rate. The building and mining industries use large quantities of wood, and the pulpwood required for one Sunday edition of the *New York Times* eats up 25 acres of forest. But the United States now grows more timber than she cuts and more and more trees are regarded as a harvest, to be cut and replanted like annual crops.

North American fishing fleets work mostly in the oceans around the continent. Their catch includes sardines, tuna, halibut, mackerel, herring, haddock and cod. The salmon fisheries of the Pacific coast are famous. Trawlers fish for cod especially in the shallow waters of the Grand Banks of Newfoundland. European ships fished in these waters long before settlers established the first permanent colonies on the mainland.

Mineral Resources and Industry

Niagara Falls: the Canadian Horseshoe Falls which are 186 feet high and 2,950 feet across at their widest point. Though the falls are most widely renowned as a tourist attraction, especially for honeymooners, their power plants are a major factor in the national economies of the United States and Canada and have played a major part in attracting industry to the surrounding region.

The United States probably produces over half of all the world's manufactured goods. North American industry has great advantages, not only in advanced management techniques, mass production, availability of skilled workers, but in the continent's natural resources. Sulfur from Louisiana, copper and salt in the Rockies, bauxite from Canada, phosphates from Florida, zinc, uranium, lead, silver, gold, nickel—in both countries—all these make North America one of the world's wealthiest areas in natural resources.

The United States produces about one seventh of the world's coal, most of it from the Appalachian field. The coal comes mainly from Pennsylvania and west Virginia where outcrops in the valley sides give the easiest possible conditions for mining.

There are also some minor coal fields supplying the Midwest in Illinois and neighboring states. The small coal fields of Wyoming and Colorado also supply local needs. The United States is the only country producing coal economically but it is facing increasing competition from other fuels. The number of miners has decreased recently but this is partly due to increased mechanization.

The United States is both the largest producer and consumer of petroleum. Oil, first tapped in western Pennsylvania a hundred years ago, brought about far-reaching changes. Gasoline powers the automobile and there are many chemical by-products of petroleum. Prospectors first struck oil in the southwest in 1901 and today the leading petroleum producing states are Texas, California, Louisiana

Modern oil refinery in Louisiana. Such refineries work for 24 hours a day processing crude oil into hundreds of different products. Petroleum and a number of chemicals are, with natural gas, the chief products of Louisiana, a state which is second only to Texas as an oil producer.

Intersecting freeways in Los Angeles. North Americans own nearly half the world total of mechanical road vehicles and are many years ahead of the rest of the world in highway construction. Engineers from all over the world come to the United States to study projects like this.

and Oklahoma. Long pipelines carry oil and natural gas from the fields to all parts of the United States. Recently the Canadians have discovered several oil fields in the Lesser Slave Lake area and Rainbow Lake region, 400 miles northwest of Edmonton.

Nearly all of Canada's electricity and one fifth of the United States' is water-generated. The United States' tapped and potential sources are the mountains of the west, the rivers of the Mississippi basin and the New England rivers. Canada's potential is concentrated in two areas—the southern half of the Shield and the mountains of British Columbia. In the United States there is a great move towards the use of atomic power in industry.

Like coal, low-grade iron ore deposits center on a single area—the ore deposits south of Lake Superior in northern Minnesota and Michigan. The ore is shipped by boat across the Great Lakes and then by train to steel centers like Pittsburgh and Chicago. More and more high-grade iron ore is coming from newly developed Canadian fields— like the one in Labrador. Around Birmingham, Alabama, there are iron ore deposits as well as coal and they form the basis of a low cost steel industry.

The first industrial centers were dependent on local supplies of power—the New England factories used water power at first; Cleveland, Pittsburgh and Birmingham grew up close to the Appalachian coalfield. As they grew, specialist industries became concentrated in certain areas; the automobile industry in southern Michigan and Ontario around Detroit; electromechanical and metallurgical industries around Buffalo, Niagara and Toronto.

Industries grew in the south and west too; away from the coal fields as new power sources like petroleum and electricity were tapped. In the areas around Puget Sound, San Francisco and Los Angeles oil refining, the aerospace industry, rubber tire manufacturing and movie and television filming are all important.

But the west coast is not alone in the development of new industries. Factories as far apart as Texas, Ontario and New England make electrical equipment, drugs, food products and plastics. Factories all over America are producing thousands of different kinds of goods every day.

The assets of industrial organization are the large size of the units, and mechanization. Most industries are dominated by a few large corporations which have a tendency to spread between the United States and Canada irrespective of the frontier.

Transportation is vital to industry. Many bulky raw materials like coal, iron ore, timber, wheat and cotton are shipped on inland waterways—traffic on the Great Lakes is mostly freight. Railroads are still the main means of transport, especially for heavy merchandise although goods are increasingly moved by road, especially in the east.

Railyards at Winnipeg, the capital of Manitoba and the "Queen City" of Canada's Prairie Provinces, the business and distributing center for Canada's big grain trade.

Life in North America

North America occupies about one sixth of the world's land surface and contains about a fifteenth of its population; but a lot of the country is still almost empty. Most Canadians live in the south. All of Alaska and most of the dry parts of the western United States have less than two people per square mile. Two thirds of Americans live in or near cities, but even the eastern United States is less crowded than comparable areas in western Europe, China or India.

When Columbus sailed, North America had only about one million people—Indians, who have lived there for over 20,000 years, and Eskimos, who crossed from Asia 2,000 years ago. Today there are 220 million people—200 million in the United States and about 20 million in Canada. This phenomenal growth is due almost entirely to the influx of immigrants.

In Canada nearly half the population is of British descent; and in east Nova Scotia and Prince Edward Island there are many descendents of the Scots who migrated there in the late 1700s and early 1800s. Many people on Cape Breton Island, off Nova Scotia, still speak Gaelic. About a third of the population is French-Canadian—some four million descendents of Frenchmen who settled in Quebec 300 years ago. Four out of five speak French, the only important official language other than English used in North America.

Since the mid-19th century over 43 million immigrants have come to America from all parts of Europe and also from China, Japan and Puerto Rico. Today five out of every 100 people living in the United States are foreign-born and 19 out of every 100 are either immigrants or children of immigrants. Ten out of every 100 are Negroes, descendents of slaves brought over from Africa in the 17th and 18th centuries. The newcomers have brought new names, styles of architecture, clothing fashions, kinds of foods, new songs and dances.

Recently most immigrants have gone to a few large cities. More than two thirds of the foreign-born now live in cities of more than a million people. New York has more Irish than Dublin, more Italians than Rome, more Greeks than Athens. Cities are constantly changing. Buildings are being demolished and rebuilt, streets are being repaved.

New York's Chinatown. The Chinese are just one of the many nationalities, about 60 in all, making up the population of New York City. Chinatown, popular with tourists, is in Lower Manhattan.

Skyscrapers have made central business areas so concentrated that congestion has become a major problem.

Americans buy more food, clothes and household goods than any other people. Six out of ten own their own homes. Many houses have air conditioning. Nearly every family has a car, refrigerator, television set and a washing machine. Americans have more than half the telephones in the world, almost half the motor vehicles and a large proportion of the private airplanes.

American farms and factories produce huge quantities of goods cheaply and efficiently, using labor-saving machinery. Much of the wheat crop is gathered by combines; automobiles roll off assembly lines; computers simplify office work. About 33 out of every 100 employed North Americans work in manufacturing and construction, and eight work in farming, fishing, forestry and mining.

High productivity means that people have more leisure time. The American industrial worker spends an average of less than 38 hours a week at his job. Household appliances and canned and frozen food make housework easier, so women have more spare time too. One in four married women also has a job.

Many people make their living by catering for leisure activities. Cities and towns maintain playgrounds, golf courses, swimming pools and parks; and great areas have been set aside as National Parks. American tourists spend more money on traveling abroad than the cost of the principal imports.

North Americans have made formidable progress in medicine and education. They have done much to promote public health programs and have made great advances in medical research. Elementary and secondary education is free; nine out of ten children go to primary school and there are more high schools in North America than in any other area. Over half a million graduate from college every year.

Canada and the United States share similar institutions of democratically elected governments, legal processes and religious beliefs. Both are federal states, where the central government is responsible for defense and foreign affairs. The individual provinces or states make their own laws governing education, transport, marriage, gambling and so on.

Rural general store. With its pot-bellied stove and genuine homeliness this is an integral part of the American way of life still surviving in the remote towns and villages.

The supermarket, successor to the old general store. Higher wages and a popular demand for the better things in life forced North America to pioneer this type of store. This typically American development has been widely adopted in Europe.

North America in World Affairs

North America is the wealthiest continent, and so inevitably exerts a tremendous economic influence in the world.

Each year the United States imports over $15 billion worth and exports over $20 billion worth of goods—about ten per cent of its total output. Almost a fifth of this trade is with Canada. Its next most important customers are Japan, Britain, West Germany and Mexico. Because of America's immense resources and great volume of trade, the United States dollar is one of the two leading currencies in the free world.

Canada imports about a third of the goods it uses and exports about a third of its output. Outside of North America, Canada's most important customer is Britain, followed by Japan, West Germany and Venezuela. Grain shipments to China and the U.S.S.R. have recently become significant sources of export income.

Both countries also export capital. North America has extensive investments in other countries, where new industry has been encouraged and old modernized.

Americans not only have a high standard of living themselves, but also provide substantial aid and technical assistance to countries in Asia, Latin America and Africa. This aid has done a lot to lessen the gap between the "have" and the "have-not" nations. The United States provides more than half the foreign aid in the world, and distributes large stocks of surplus agricultural products to the developing countries under its Food for Peace program. American Peace Corps and Canadian University Service Overseas volunteers work in 47 countries, assisting in educational and technical development projects. Canada and the United States are both members of the Colombo Plan, which helps economic progress in southern and southeast Asia.

Canada, as a member of the British Commonwealth, has a special relationship with the United Kingdom. It also has historic cultural links with France. The United States is generally regarded as the leader of the western nations and the guardian

Wall Street, New York, financial center of the western world. The Dow Jones Index reflecting the price level on the Wall Street stockmarket is watched closely in all the European capitals.

of democracy; in this role it took up arms in Korea, with other United Nations forces, and in Vietnam. Canada also sent troops to Korea. Both countries are members of the United Nations. The United States has a permanent seat on the Security Council and contributes about a third of the total U.N. budget. Both also belong to the North Atlantic Treaty Organization (N.A.T.O.). The United States inspired the Organization of American States and the Alliance for Progress, a development program for Latin America. It belongs to the South East Asia Treaty Organization (S.E.A.T.O.) and, although not a member, takes part in the Central Treaty Organization (C.E.N.T.O.).

North American contributions to the arts have won worldwide recognition. American writing has influenced the development of new literary forms. The West has inspired its own ballads, as distinctly American as jazz; and both have influenced modern classical music. Artists and architects have helped develop contemporary design trends.

The telephone and the electric light are part of a long American tradition of invention and technological development. Plastics, synthetic fibers, computers, automation and mass production techniques —all these affect the way the rest of the world lives. Almost half a million scientists, backed by an increasing research program, are finding new cures for disease, discovering more about the structure of the atom and the chemistry of heredity; and are working closely with other countries in ocean and radio astronomy studies. Basic genetics research in the United States has greatly increased the world's supply of food, developing new strains like hybrid corn. United States space probes have added to knowledge about the earth and universe. Relay satellites have revolutionized global radio and television communication.

North Americans, with their vigor, vast economic resources, political influence and concern for the people of other countries, are taking their full share of responsibility for the future welfare of the world.

Royal Avenue in New Orleans. The decorative ironwork on the balconies is typical of the French quarter in this, the largest city of Louisiana. New Orleans is a marketing center for cotton, cottonseed oil and rice. One of the world's great ports, it also has nearly 1000 manufacturing and processing plants. Everyone knows its place in the history of jazz.

A Peace Corps teacher with her English class in the girls secondary school at Kabul, Afghanistan. Like many others from the United States, she volunteered to work in all corners of the world outside of the Communist countries.

COUNTRIES OF NORTH AMERICA

 UNITED STATES OF AMERICA*
Republic
N. America
Area: 3,615,000 sq. miles

Pop: 200,000,000. **Land use** %: grassland 34; forest 32; cultivated 24; waste 10. **Occupations:** manufacturing, services, commerce, agriculture, fishing, forestry. **Industries:** iron and steel, heavy engineering, atomic power, aircraft, automobiles, electrical equipment, food products. **Capital:** Washington D.C. (764,000; metropolitan statistical area 2,408,000). **Largest cities:** (with populations of city proper and urbanized area): New York City (7,782,000; 14,115,000), Los Angeles (2,479,000; 6,489,000), Chicago (3,550,000; 5,959,000), Philadelphia (1,003,000; 3,635,000), Detroit (1,670,000; 3,538,000). **Overseas Responsibilities:** Puerto Rico—commonwealth associated with the United States; Virgin Islands of the United States—unincorporated territory; Guam—unincorporated territory; American Samoa—unincorporated territory; Trust Territory of the Pacific Islands—trusteeship for the United Nations; Panama Canal Zone—United States government reservation; Corn Islands—leased from Nicaragua; Pacific Islands under U.S. control. (Ryukyu Islands, Daito Islands, Bonin Islands, Volcano Islands).

1 UNITED STATES OF AMERICA
2 CANADA

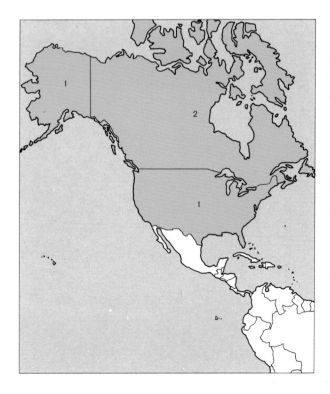

* Member of the United Nations

State	Nickname	Date Admitted Union	Ad-mission	Pop.	Capital	Flower	Tree	Bird	Song
Alabama (51,609 sq.mi.)	Heart of Dixie, Cotton State	Dec. 14, 1819	22	3,517,000	Montgomery	Camellia	Southern (Longleaf) Pine	Yellow-hammer	"Alabama"
Alaska (586,400 sq. mi.)	—	Jan. 3, 1959	49	272,000	Juneau	Forget-me-not	Sitka Spruce	Willow Ptarmigan	"Alaska's Flag"
Arizona (113,909 sq. mi.)	Grand Canyon State	Feb. 14, 1912	48	1,618,000	Phoenix	Giant Cactus or Saguaro	Paloverde	Cactus Wren	"Arizona"
Arkansas (53,104 sq. mi.)	Land of Opportunity	June 15, 1836	25	1,955,000	Little Rock	Apple Blossom	Shortleaf Pine	Mocking Bird	"Arkansas"
California (158,693 sq.mi.)	Golden State	Sept. 9, 1850	31	18,918,000	Sacramento	California Poppy	Redwood	Valley Quail	"I Love You, California"
Colorado (104,247 sq.mi.)	Centennial State	Aug. 1, 1876	38	1,977,000	Denver	Columbine	Colorado Blue Spruce	Lark Bunting	"Where the Columbines Grow"
Connecticut (5,009 sq. mi.)	Nutmeg State Constitution State	1788	5	2,875,000	Hartford	Mountain Laurel	White Oak	American Robin	—
Delaware (2,057 sq.mi.)	First State. Diamond State	1787	1	512,000	Dover	Peach Blossom	American Holly	Blue Hen Chicken	"Our Delaware"
Florida (58,560 sq. mi.)	Sunshine State	May 3, 1845	27	5,941,000	Tallahassee	Orange Blossom	Sabal Palm	Mocking Bird	"The Swanee River"
Georgia (58,876 sq.mi.)	Empire State of the South, Peach State	1788	4	4,459,000	Atlanta	Cherokee Rose	Live Oak	Brown Thrasher	"Georgia"
Hawaii (6,424 sq.mi.)	Aloha State	Mar. 11 and 12, 1959	50	718,000	Honolulu	Hibiscus	Kukui (Candlenut)	Nene (Hawaiian Goose)	"Hawaii Ponoi" (unofficial)
Idaho (83,557 sq.mi.)	Gem State	July 3, 1890	43	694,000	Boise	Lewis Mock Orange	Western White Pine	Mountain Bluebird	"Here We Have Idaho"
Illinois (56,400 sq.mi.)	Prairie State	Dec. 3, 1818	21	10,722,000	Springfield	Butterfly Violet	Bur Oak	Cardinal	"Illinois"
Indiana (36,291 sq.mi.)	Hoosier State	Dec. 11, 1816	19	4,918,000	Indianapolis	Peony	Tulip (Yellow Poplar)	Cardinal	"On the Banks of the Wabash"
Iowa (56,290 sq.mi.)	Hawkeye State	Dec. 28, 1846	29	2,747,000	Des Moines	Wild Rose	Oak	Eastern Goldfinch	"Iowa"
Kansas (82,264 sq.mi.)	Sunflower State	Jan. 29, 1861	34	2,250,000	Topeka	Sunflower	Cottonwood	Western Meadow Lark	"Home on the Range"
Kentucky (40,395 sq.mi.)	Blue Grass State	June 1, 1792	15	3,183,000	Frankfort	Goldenrod	Tuliptree	Cardinal	"My Old Kentucky Home"
Louisiana (48,523 sq.mi.)	Pelican State	Apr. 30, 1812	18	3,603,000	Baton Rouge	Magnolia Grandiflora	Bald Cypress	Eastern Brown Pelican	"Song of Louisiana"
Maine (33,215 sq.mi.)	Pine Tree State	Mar. 15, 1820	23	983,000	Augusta	Pine Cone and Tassel	Eastern White Pine	Chickadee	"State of Maine Song"

State	Nickname	Date Admitted	Ad-mission	Pop.	Capital	Flower	Tree	Bird	Song
Maryland (10,577 sq.mi.)	Old Line State, Free State	1788	7	3,613,000	Annapolis	Black-eyed Susan	White Oak	Baltimore	"Maryland, My Maryland"
Massachusetts (8,257 sq.mi.)	Bay State, Old Colony	1788	6	5,383,000	Boston	Mayflower	American Elm	Chickadee	"Massa-chusetts" (unofficial)
Michigan (58,216 sq.mi.)	Wolverine State	Jan. 26, 1837	26	8,374,000	Lansing	Apple Blossom	White Pine	Robin	"My Michigan" (unofficial)
Minnesota (84,068 sq.mi.)	North Star State, Gopher State	May 11, 1858	32	3,576,000	St. Paul	Showy Lady's-slipper	Red (Nor-way) Pine	Loon	"Hail! Minnesota"
Mississippi (47,716 sq.mi.)	Magnolia State	Dec. 10, 1817	20	2,327,000	Jackson	Magnolia	Magnolia	Mocking Bird	"Go, Miss-issippi"
Missouri (69,686 sq.mi.)	Show Me State	Aug. 10, 1821	24	4,508,000	Jefferson City	Hawthorn	Dogwood	Eastern Bluebird	"Missouri Waltz"
Montana (147,138 sq.mi.)	Treasure State	Nov. 8, 1889	41	702,000	Helena	Bitterroot Lewisia	Ponderosa Pine	Western Meadow Lark	"Montana"
Nebraska (77,227 sq.mi.)	Beef State, Corn-husker State	Mar. 1, 1867	37	1,456,000	Lincoln	Goldenrod	American Elm	Western Meadow Lark	—
Nevada (110,540 sq.mi.)	Sagebrush State, Silver State	Oct. 31, 1864	36	454,000	Carson City	Sagebrush	Single-leaf Piñon	Mountain Bluebird	"Home Means Nevada"
New Hampshire (9,304 sq.mi.)	Granite State	June 21, 1788	9	681,000	Concord	Common Lilac	Paper (White) Birch	Purple Finch	"Old New Hamp-shire"
New Jersey (7,836 sq.mi.)	Garden State	1787	3	6,898,000	Trenton	Purple Violet	Red Oak	Eastern Goldfinch	—
New Mexico (121,666 sq.mi.)	Land of Enchant-ment	Jan. 6, 1912	47	1,022,000	Santa Fe	Yucca	Piñon (Nut Pine)	Road Runner	"O, Fair New Mexico"
New York (49,576 sq.mi.)	Empire State	1788	11	18,258,000	Albany	Rose	Sugar Maple	Eastern Bluebird	—
North Carolina (52,712 sq.mi.)	Tar Heel State, Old North State	1789	12	5,000,000	Raleigh	Dogwood	Pine	Cardinal	"The Old North State"
North Dakota (70,665 sq.mi.)	Sioux State, Flickertail State	Nov. 2, 1889	39 or 40	650,000	Bismarck	Wild Prairie Rose	American Elm	Western Meadow Lark	"North Da-kota Hymn"
Ohio (41,222 sq.mi.)	Buckeye State	Feb. 19, 1803	17	10,305,000	Columbus	Scarlet Carnation	Ohio Buckeye	Cardinal	
Oklahoma (69,919 sq.mi.)	Sooner State	Nov. 16, 1907	46	2,458,000	Oklahoma City	Mistletoe	Redbud	Scissor-tailed Flycatcher	"Oklahoma"
Oregon (96,981 sq.mi.)	Beaver State	Feb. 14, 1859	33	1,955,000	Salem	Oregon Grape	Douglas Fir	Western Meadow Lark	"Oregon, My Oregon"
Pennsylvania (45,333 sq.mi.)	Keystone State	1787	2	11,582,000	Harrisburg	Mountain Laurel	Eastern Hemlock	Ruffed Grouse	—
Rhode Island (1,214 sq.mi.)	Little Rhody	1790	13	898,000	Providence	Violet	Red Maple	Rhode Island Red	"Rhode Island"
S. Carolina (31,055 sq.mi.)	Palmetto State	1788	8	2,586,000	Columbia	Carolina (Yellow) Jessamine	Cabbage Palmetto	Carolina Wren	"Carolina"
S. Dakota (77,047 sq.mi.)	Coyote State, Sunshine State	Nov. 2, 1889	39 or 40	682,000	Pierre	Pasque	Black Hills Spruce	Ringnecked Pheasant	"Hail South Dakota"
Tennessee (42,244 sq.mi.)	Volunteer State	June 1, 1796	16	3,883,000	Nashville	Iris	Tulip Poplar	Mocking-bird	"When it's Iris Time In Tennessee"
Texas (267,339 sq.mi.)	Lone Star State	Dec. 29, 1845	28	10,752,000	Austin	Bluebonnet	Pecan	Mocking-bird	"Texas, Our Texas"

State	Nickname	Date Admitted	Ad-mission	Pop.	Capital	Flower	Tree	Bird	Song
Utah (84,916 sq.mi.)	Beehive State	Jan. 4, 1896	45	1,008,000	Salt Lake City	Sego Lily	Blue Spruce	California Gull	"Utah, We Love Thee"
Vermont (9,609 sq.mi.)	Green Mountain State	Mar. 4, 1791	14	405,000	Montpelier	Red Clover	Sugar Maple	Hermit Thrush	"Hail, Vermont"
Virginia (40,817 sq.mi.)	Old Dominion	1788	10	4,507,000	Richmond	American Dogwood	American Dogwood (unofficial)	Cardinal	"Carry Me Back To Old Virginia"
Washington (68,192 sq.mi.)	Evergreen State	Nov. 11, 1889	42	2,980,000	Olympia	Coast Rhododen-dron	Western Hemlock	Willow Goldfinch	"Washing-ton, My Home"
W. Virginia (24,181 sq.mi.)	Mountain State	June 20, 1863	35	1,794,000	Charleston	Rosebay Rhododen-dron max.	Sugar Maple	Cardinal	"West Vir-ginia, My Home,Sweet Home"
Wisconsin (56,154 sq.mi.)	Badger State	May 29, 1848	30	4,161,000	Madison	Wood Violet	Sugar Maple	Robin	"On, Wis-consin"
Wyoming (97,914 sq.mi.)	Equality State	July 10, 1890	44	329,000	Cheyenne	Indian Paintbrush	Cottonwood (Balsam Poplar)	Western Meadow Lark	—
District of Columbia (67 sq.mi.)	—	—	—	808,000	—	American Beauty Rose	Scarlet Oak	Wood Thrush	—

CANADA* †
Constitutional Monarchy
N. America
Area: 3,852,000 sq. miles

Pop: 20,346,000. **Land use** %: waste 58; forest 35; cultivated 4; grassland 3. **Occupations:** manufacturing, agriculture, forestry, hunting, fishing, government services, mining. **Industries:** mineral refining, wood pulp and paper, food canning, processing agricultural products, consumer goods. **Capital:** Ottawa (268,206; metropolitan area 495,000). **Largest cities** (with population of city proper and metropolitan area): Montreal (1,191,000; 2,437,000), Toronto (672,000; 2,158,000), Vancouver (385,000; 892,000).

Province	Date Admitted Dominion	Area	Population	Capital	Floral Emblem	Motto
Newfoundland	1949	156,185	493,396	St. John's	Pitcher Plant	Seek Ye First the Kingdom of God
Prince Edward Island	1873	2,184	108,535	Charlottetown	Lady's Slipper	The Small Under the Protection of the Great
Nova Scotia	1867	21,425	756,039	Halifax	Mayflower	One Defends & the Other Conquers
New Brunswick	1867	28,354	616,788	Fredericton	Purple Violet	—
Quebec	1867	594,860	5,780,845	Quebec	White Garden Lily	I Remember
Ontario	1867	412,582	6,960,870	Toronto	White Trillium	Loyal in the Beginning, So It Remained
Manitoba	1870	251,000	963,066	Winnipeg	Prairie Crocus	—
Saskatchewan	1905	251,700	955,344	Regina	Prairie Lily	—
Alberta	1905	255,285	1,463,203	Edmonton	Wild Rose	—
British Columbia	1871	366,255	1,873,674	Victoria	Pacific Dogwood	Splendor Without Diminish-ment
Territories						
Yukon Territory		207,076	14,382	Whitehorse	Fireweed	—
Northwest Territories		1,304,903	28,738	Yellowknife	Mountain Avens	—

* Member of the United Nations
† Member of the British Commonwealth

Andean landscape. The Andes extend along the whole Pacific coast of South America from Cape Horn in the south to Venezuela in the north, a distance of about 4,500 miles. They are the longest mountain system in the world. Their snow-capped peaks include Aconcagua (22,834 feet), the highest in the western hemisphere. The central Andes of Bolivia and Peru have many high plateaus, and are the home of the Inca empire and other ancient cultures.

LATIN AMERICAN LANDS

This vast region of mountain and plain, where much of the land is still uncultivated, can be divided geographically into Middle America and South America. Lying mostly in the tropics, it contains dense forests, rich grasslands, rainless deserts, active and dormant volcanoes. Along the west coast earthquakes are frequent. Its natural resources are as varied as its climates.

Middle American Countries

Today Middle America is most widely known as a colorful holiday paradise, dotted with banana and sugar cane plantations, the air filled with the throb of steel bands and the gay music of calypso songs. Here 20,000 years ago the Mayan and Aztec civilizations grew and flourished. Here, too, came the stately Spanish galleons drawing pirates behind them with a golden magnet.

This region of hurricanes and palm trees, legends and oil derricks, includes Mexico, the Central American land bridge and the island arcs of the West Indies. It is one of the world's most crowded areas, supporting three per cent of all the people on earth on less than two per cent of the total global cultivated area.

Mexico is the most important country in Middle America. The north region is a plateau penned in by mountains, open to cold, dry prevailing winds. The mountains of the narrow, arid California peninsula and the Western Sierra Madre are continuations of the Pacific ranges of the United States. The Eastern Sierra Madre, about 10,000 feet high, is an extension of the Rockies. Between the two Sierras lies the Mexican Plateau, rising from 3,600 feet near the United States border to 8,000 feet near

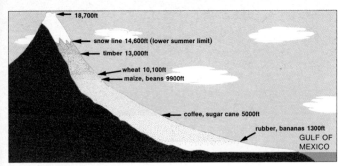

Diagram showing the vegetation zones on the eastern slope of Mount Citlalteptl, Mexico. The arrows show heights which are the upper limits of growth for all the plants named.

18,700ft
snow line 14,600ft (lower summer limit)
timber 13,000ft
wheat 10,100ft
maize, beans 9900ft
coffee, sugar cane 5000ft
rubber, bananas 1300ft
GULF OF MEXICO

Mexico City. An east-west line of volcanic mountains, some over 17,000 feet high, like Popocatepetl, lies south of Mexico City; and plains border the sea on both coasts.

Mountains run south of Mexico through Guatemala, British Honduras, El Salvador, Nicaragua, Costa Rica and Panama; all hot, humid countries with dense tropical forests.

The Greater and Lesser Antilles curve in two arcs in the Caribbean. These islands are popular winter resorts since the weather is mild. Surface temperatures of Caribbean water are always above 68°F., so many of the islands are coral; since polyps can only live in warm water. Temperatures along the coast average between 70°F. and 85°F., but they decrease with altitude in the mountainous interiors.

The rainy season lasts from August to October, when 60–70 inches of rain falls in violent showers, heaviest on the windward side of the islands (usually the northeast or east). The difference in the amount which falls on the two sides of mountainous islands like Jamaica or Puerto Rico may be as much as 200 inches. Most harbors and towns grew up on the lee sides of the islands, safe from huge waves and strong winds. Hurricanes are frequent and sweep across the West Indies and Gulf of Mexico, causing great destruction. They usually occur in August and continue to be a threat during September and October.

The Caribbean coasts of South America, Panama and Costa Rica lie outside the hurricane area. Here, temperature varies with altitude. Rain falls all year —an average of 100 inches. Elsewhere in Central America the heaviest rain is in summer.

Altitude also determines Mexico's climate. Below 3,000 feet temperatures range between 70°F. in January and 80°F. in July. Rain falls mostly in

Rain forest in Haiti. Dense forests like this are typical in the mountainous volcanic islands of the Caribbean, especially on their east coasts where the trade winds bring in dense rain clouds from the Atlantic. The average rainfall over Haiti and the neighboring Dominican Republic, is from 40 to 80 inches a year.

132

The famous "Floating Gardens" or *chinampas* of Xochimilco, a town about 10 miles south of Mexico City on the small and shallow Lake Xochimilco. The gardens are really small artificial islands in a maze of waterways.

summer; more than 100 inches annually in the tropical lowlands bordering the Gulf of Mexico but less than 20 in the north of the plateau and as little as 2 in the Sonora.

Natural vegetation reflects climate changes. The north Mexican plateau is covered with cacti and low mesquite and sagebrush like the southwestern United States. Forests cover Mexico's mountains and plains; the trees are mostly hardwoods like ebony and walnut. The West Indies have tropical forests containing valuable hardwood, though scrub grasses cover limestone-soil areas. Palm trees grow on the low coral islands.

Giant cactus plant in the Sonora Desert through which the United States-Mexican border runs. Plants like these are well adapted to desert conditions. They can take in and store more than 650 gallons of water during the short rainy season.

South American Countries

Rio de Janeiro by night. Brazil's second largest city, Rio stands on Guanabara Bay. Its most famous landmarks are the Sugar Loaf, a peak 1,230 feet high rising from the bay, and the statue of Christ the Redeemer on Corcovado Mountain (2,310 feet). The city is an important industrial center and seaport, and was capital of Brazil until 1960, when the new city of Brasilia was made the capital. (This picture is published by courtesy of Pan American Airlines.)

The Andes mountain system, the South American equivalent of the Rockies, molds the western coast of this continent. South America also has mountains on the east and central plains like North America. But nearly three quarters of South America lies within the Tropics and so it does not have so stimulating climate as its northern neighbor.

The Andes are much narrower than the Rockies but also much higher, with many peaks over 20,000 feet. Rugged, snow-capped mountains with glaciers sliding slowly down their sides rise above the narrow coastal plain to the west. Some mountains are volcanic and earthquakes often shake this region. The Andean Range extends right from Tierra del Fuego —the southern tip of South America—north through the broadest part in Bolivia, where there is a wide plateau between bordering mountain chains; and curves around in a great arc ending at Trinidad. In the whole of this range, altitude rather than latitude has the most effect on climate.

To the east of the Andes, three plains less than 600 feet above sea level spread across the continent. In the north is the huge basin of the River Amazon, one of the longest rivers in the world. The Amazon rises in the Peruvian Andes and winds a tortuous course right across the continent to the Atlantic Ocean, a distance of more than 3,000 miles. The river is building a large delta out into the sea, discoloring the water, and carrying fresh water, as far as 200 miles out. In the days of sail one skipper, out of water and well out of the sight of land, hoisted a distress signal off the mouth of the Amazon to enlist the aid of a passing coaster: "Help. We need water". Back came the reply: "Lower your buckets".

For thousands of years the Amazon and its tributaries have been wearing away the highlands and building up extensive alluvial plains. Equatorial rain forests or *selvas* cover the Amazon basin, since this region is always hot and humid.

The divide between the Amazon Plain and the Orinoco Plains in the north is very low at one point. Here the Casiquiare River sometimes flows into the Negro, a tributary of the Amazon, and sometimes into the Orinoco. The Orinoco basin has a dry season and a wet season; and tropical grasses grow here. These grassy plains are called *llanos*.

South of the Amazon Basin are three lowland areas crossed by rivers, making up the Parana-Paraguay Plains. The Gran Chaco of Argentina and Paraguay, partly forested scrubland, has a tropical climate with high temperatures and low rainfall. South of the Gran Chaco the *pampas* of Argentina is warm, temperate grassland. 20–40 inches of rain falls a year, with a maximum in summer. This kind of climate is suitable for farming and ranching and the pampas is one of the world's largest meat producing areas. East of these regions the Entre Rios has a humid climate only slightly cooler than the Orinoco Plains in the north.

The Guinea Highlands along Brazil's northern boundary are less than 5,000 feet high. The Brazilian Highlands rise steeply to over 9,000 feet along the Atlantic coast. They have a tropical climate with a maximum rainfall in summer. In southern Argentina the Patagonian Plateaus form tablelands ending in steep cliffs along the Atlantic. From the sea they rise like giant "steps", the highest over 5,000 feet above sea level. These tablelands are cool, dry and wind-swept, but they form one of the world's largest sheep-grazing areas in spite of the fact that the grass crop is sparse. They are crossed by deep east-west canyons.

A fringe of coastal lowland along the Pacific Ocean lies west of the Andes. It is very narrow everywhere except in Chile, where a lowland area between the mountains stretches south from Santiago. At Puerto Montt melting waters at the end of the last Ice Age flooded the lower part of this valley.

These narrow coastal plains bordering the Pacific can be divided according to climate. Temperatures get warmer towards the Equator but latitude for latitude the temperatures are lower than in other parts of the world. This is not only because the off-shore Humboldt has cold waters but also because close to the coast cooler waters still well up from below the surface. In Colombia and Ecuador the coastal plains are swampy with tropical forests. Farther south the hot dry area of the Atacama Desert has less than 10 inches of rain a year. The dry belt swings right across the Andes into Patagonia. Middle Chile has a Mediterranean climate with mild winters and dry summers, and southern Chile has a climate like the coasts of the state of Washington and British Columbia, with heavy rainfall due to the westerly winds.

Top: equatorial rain forest in the Amazon basin. This vast area is almost uninhabited except by Indians. Other Brazilians prefer to live in those parts of their enormous country which are easier to clear and develop.

Below: sheep station in Tierra del Fuego, a group of islands at the southern tip of South America. The rancher has burned the ground deliberately and sown grass seed in the hot ashes to increase the pasturage.

South America

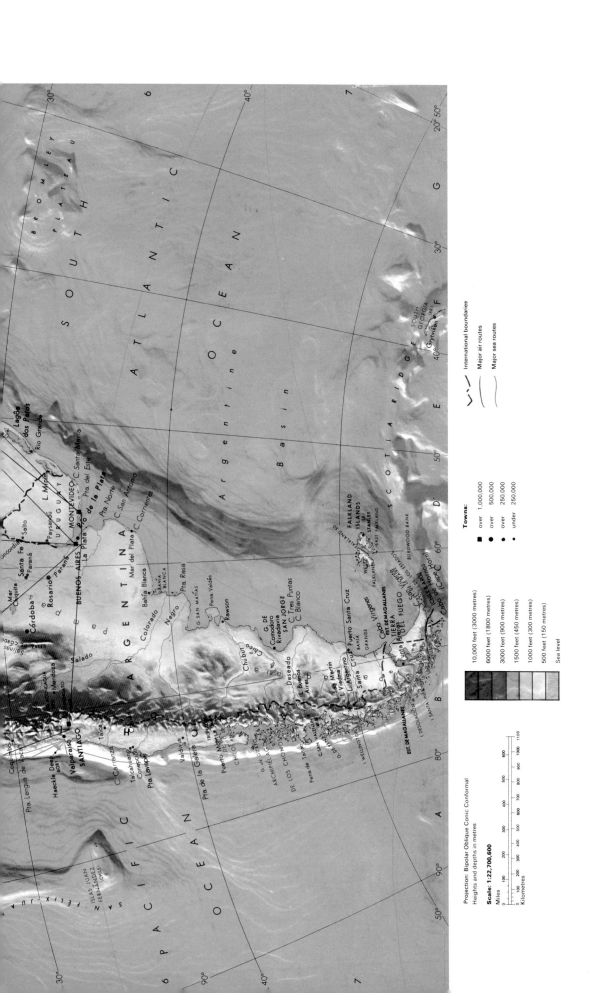

Projection: Bipolar Oblique Conic Conformal

Heights and depths in metres

Scale: 1:22,700,600

Miles
```
0  100  200  300  400  500  600
```

Kilometres
```
0  100  200  300  400  500  600  700  800  900  1000  1100
```

Towns:

■ over 1,000,000
● over   500,000
• over   250,000
· under   250,000

10,000 feet (3000 metres)
6000 feet (1800 metres)
3000 feet (900 metres)
1500 feet (450 metres)
1000 feet (300 metres)
500 feet (150 metres)
Sea level

⌒⌒ International boundaries
⌒   Major air routes
⌒   Major sea routes

Latin America: Natural Resources

Top: an Indian of the Peruvian Andes where the simple way of life has probably changed little over the years and is based on primitive farming. Potatoes, corn, barley and a herb called *ocas* are the main foods. Nearly half the population of Peru is of pure Indian (Quechua or Aymara) descent.
Below: harvesting sugar cane in Jamaica with the machete, a razor-sharp sword-like knife. Most of the workers on plantations in the Caribbean are Negroes.

Gold was one of the main reasons for the Spanish conquest of Latin America. But Middle and South America have a large variety of other minerals, unevenly distributed but forming one of the region's principal assets. A lot of mineral wealth lies untouched either because it is too remote or because countries in this part of the world lack capital for exploitation.

Apart from petroleum, most of which goes for exports, Latin America has few power reserves. There are small coal deposits in many places, including Brazil and Chile; but only Colombia, with reserves near Bogotá, mines coal on any scale. Some countries have been able to develop hydroelectric power. South Mexico and Central America, with short, fast-flowing rivers, have hydroelectric stations that supply a lot of their electricity requirement. But Brazil and Venezuela have the greatest hydroelectric power potential in South America. The Quiroz scheme in Peru will provide water for irrigation and power.

Petroleum is found near the Andean fold mountains, especially in the north where the ranges swing east to Trinidad. Petroleum has made Venezuela's fortune. She is the third largest producer in the world and the biggest exporter. Mexico is also a leading producer of oil and natural gas. Argentina and Chile are self-sufficient in petroleum. Trinidad, Colombia, Peru and Ecuador are also producers.

Like the Rockies in North America, the Andes and Mexican Sierras are rich sources of a wide variety of non-ferrous minerals, like silver, lead, copper, zinc, platinum and tin. The world demand for copper outstrips supply, so Chile's reserves (one third of the world's total) are highly valuable. Chile's annual output is half that of the United States, and she also refines copper.

Tin forms the basis of Bolivia's economy. She is third among the world's producers. Recent exploration has also uncovered vast gold reserves in Bolivia. Mexico is a leading producer of silver, lead and zinc, and has large undeveloped reserves of iron ore. Most Mexican mines are foreign-owned.

Some countries have deposits of minerals used in nuclear fuels: Brazil, Argentina, Mexico and Peru mine thorium, and Brazil also has uranium deposits. Jamaica is the world's largest bauxite producer and exports a lot in the form of alumina to Canada and Scandinavia; Guyana also mines bauxite. Iron ore deposits in Venezuela, Brazil and Chile are the

Top: Argentine gaucho driving cattle on the Pampas (grassy plains). Argentina, whose wealth is based on its great cattle industry, is the world's largest exporter of beef.
Below: sugar barge at Maceió, capital of the maritime state of Alagoas, northeastern Brazil. The main port installations are at Jaraguá, the commercial center, one mile from the capital. Both sugar and cotton are leading exports of Brazil.

basis of their iron and steel industries. South America may become self-sufficient in steel; she has many minerals available for making alloys.

In spite of this great mineral wealth, more than half the people of Latin America make their living from agriculture; though a lot of potentially rich agricultural land is exhausted and soil erosion is a constant problem. But there are many estates that grow commercial crops for export—sugar, coffee, bananas and wheat. The great plains are ideal for beef and sheep ranching. But a region that could be self-supporting in food has to import some produce. The large holdings which do produce food are in the hands of a few and the small farmer who should be producing the extra food is too undereducated and undercapitalized to do so.

Forests probably cover one third of the land, but most of them are mixed and difficult to work. Fire, erosion and primitive forestry methods have already depleted the most accessible.

Peruvian waters abound with fish, and fishing is one of the country's main industries. The rate of expansion since 1958 has been high and Peru is now the world's leading fishing nation, with an annual catch of nearly seven million tons. Fishmeal and other fish products are now Peru's most valuable export, large quantities being taken by West Germany, the Netherlands, the United Kingdom and the United States. But Latin Americans are not great fish eaters—probably as fishing methods are backward and there is no refrigeration.

Life in Latin American Lands

Latin America covers nearly one fifth of the world's land surface and sprawls across a wide range of latitude. Today the population is about 248 million but by the year 2000 experts estimate it will have doubled.

About 168 million people live in South America but this is less crowded than Middle America. Most people in South America live near the coast. Hardly anyone lives in the extreme south or in the central region around the Amazon Basin. So pressure on resources is greater in Middle America and people tend to emigrate from this region, like the Puerto Ricans who go mainly to New York, and Jamaicans to Britain. South America is a region of immigration. Only about one third of Latin Americans live in large cities like Lima, Recife, Buenos Aires, Havana and Mexico City.

The three main strains in Latin America's population are the American Indian, Iberian (Spanish or Portuguese) and African (Negro). Many people are of mixed descent. The Indians were the native people of the Americas. Their ancestors came from Asia across the narrow Bering Strait separating the two continents 20,000 years ago. When the Portuguese colonized the coastal regions of what is now Brazil, the Indian population was unwilling to work for them. So the Portuguese brought in Negro slave labor from the Guinea coast of Africa to work in their plantations. Today Brazil is indifferent to the questions of color in her population. Similarly the Spaniards established plantations in Middle America using imported labor. In the 17th century the British, French and Dutch started plantations (especially sugar) in Latin America with African slave labor. Later some Asians too came to work on the plantations.

Latin America has a total pure native Indian population of 20 million. Most of them live in Bolivia, Ecuador, Guatemala and Peru. Negroes predominate in the West Indies; Negroes and people of mixed African, white and Indian ancestry make up majority groups in the Dominican Republic, Haiti and Panama. White people form

Mexicans, each with a crown of thorns, at a pilgrimage. Nine out of ten of all Latin Americans are Roman Catholics so religious festivals play an important part in their lives. Most towns and villages hold an annual *fiesta* to honor their patron saints.

Above: Palace of the Dawn, the official residence of the president at Brasilia, the capital of Brazil, was designed by the distinguished Brazilian architect Oscar Niemeyer. This remarkable city is about 600 miles northwest of Rio de Janeiro, the old capital.

Right: Brazilians enjoy celebrations and festivals. Biggest of all is the pre-Lent *Carnaval* in Rio de Janeiro. The city is decorated, colorful costumes are worn, and for four days and nights the streets are given over to parades, music and dancing.

most of the population of Argentina, Brazil, Costa Rica and Uruguay. *Mestizos* (people of mixed Indian and Iberian descent) make up Latin America's largest population group. *Mulattoes* are people of Iberian-African descent and people of Indian and African descent are called *zambos* or *cafusos*.

Many Latin Americans speak Spanish and Portuguese and some speak French. A lot of the Indians speak only the language or dialect of their tribe.

Latin Americans generally have a poor standard of living. Although many parts of the region are endowed with good soils and mineral resources, the countries employ backward farming methods and lack both the capital and the will to exploit their natural resources. Most Latin Americans experience great hardship. Many people go hungry and live in poor houses without amenities. A majority of the population make their living from the land even though only a small proportion of the region is cultivated. Most of the agricultural population are tenant farmers. Land ownership is often in the hands of a few wealthy families, but to carry out land reform programs governments need capital to buy the land. The drift of population to the towns creates slums. But the centers of many Latin American cities look very much like those of the United States with apartment blocks, busy roads and parks.

The great problem in Latin America is illiteracy. All countries now provide free schooling in theory but still there is a great shortage of schools and teachers. In Bolivia, Guatemala and Honduras only 40 per cent of the population can read and write. Some countries have made great strides in education; like Argentina, Costa Rica and Uruguay, where about 85 per cent of the people are literate. Another difficulty occurs where parents expect their children to work to help support the family.

By the early 1600's Spanish and Portuguese had colonized most of Latin America. During the nineteenth century these colonies fought for and won their independence. Since then the countries have largely been ruled by military dictatorships, with the result that changes of government have tended to occur only by force. In Communist Cuba, a strict dictatorship has governed the country since the revolution of 1959.

A new and unpredictable factor in Latin America's future has been operating since 1950 when large numbers of young Japanese peasants began emigrating to Brazil.

Latin America and the World

Latin America is a producer and exporter of primary products: agricultural produce like coffee, bananas, linseed, sunflower seeds, sugar, cocoa, meat, wool and wheat; and a wide variety of minerals like gold, copper, silver, tin and petroleum. The agricultural products are mainly foodstuffs, more than half coming from the tropics. Many national economies depend on the sale of a single cash crop. In 1965 the Cuban sugar crop was her third largest but a lot of the crop was unsold because of a glut in the world market.

In their trade with one another, Latin American nations have tried to reduce the tariff barriers. The South American countries and Mexico formed the Latin American Free Trade Association. And the Central American Common Market (Guatemala, El Salvador, Honduras, Nicaragua, Costa Rica) is one of the fastest-growing areas in Latin America.

The United States looms large on Latin American horizons not only as a trading partner but also as a provider of financial aid and technological know-how. More than 50 per cent of Latin America's exports go to the United States, which supplies 70 per cent of the region's imports. The Spanish-speaking countries of Middle America like Costa Rica and El Salvador sell to the United States the tropical crops she cannot grow herself. The great wheat and meat producing nations, Argentina and Uruguay, are having difficulty in finding markets for their primary products—complicated by the fact that in Argentina foot and mouth disease among cattle is found everywhere, and so many European countries have closed their doors to Argentinian meat to keep their own stock healthy. The United States does not need wheat and meat imports. Argentina is now sending wheat to new markets—the U.S.S.R., China and Italy—but still she cannot sell all her crop.

Great Britain and West Germany, the largest European buyers of Latin American products, take about 10 per cent of the region's exports and supply the same percentage of imports. Trade with Communist states is on the increase. The Soviet bloc takes two thirds of Cuba's exports.

It is very much in the interests of the United States that Latin America remains a peacefully developing region. The United States has given assistance to Latin America to help economic and social development programs. These activities are focused in the Organization of American States. The O.A.S. was set up to foster mutual understanding and cooperation between the states of the

A girl of the primitive Karajà tribe, which lives on the banks of the Araguia River in the *selvas* (equatorial rain forest) of the Amazon basin in Brazil. She is painting a tribal dancer with the traditional dyes of the region made from forest plants and mosses.

Americas. Cuba, which receives aid from the Soviet Union, is not a member; neither are the British Commonwealth countries of Jamaica, British Honduras, Trinidad and Tobago, and Guyana. Private American and European companies too have developed many mining and manufacturing industries in Latin America.

In spite of assistance from outside there is a general shortage of trained scientific and technological personnel in Latin America. But Latin American governments can obtain experts to advise on sanitary, educational and agricultural programs from the O.A.S.; and some research and experiments carried out by Latin Americans themselves have been notably successful, particularly in the field of animal breeding. Brazilian breeders have successfully crossed Holstein-Friesian and Hereford cattle from Denmark, the Netherlands and Great Britain, with the humped Brahman stock from India. The European strain ensures good milk yields while the Brahman provides the necessary stamina

Top: gas collection station on Lake Maracaibo, Venezuela. The lake is the center of a rich oil and natural gas region; and the city of Maracaibo, on the channel connecting the lake with the Gulf of Venezuela, is one of the world's most important petroleum export centers. Venezuela is the world's largest exporter of petroleum and the third largest producer.

National University in Mexico City. Founded in 1552, it has more than 40,000 students. Education, especially in science and technology, is Latin America's biggest need. Even Mexico, where education is free and compulsory till the age of 15, has not enough schools for all to attend.

for tropical grassland conditions. Research into pest control and use of insecticides has already increased crop yields.

Music is by far the most popular of the arts in Latin America. We take the tango from Argentina and the samba from Brazil. Composers of serious music have won fame all over the world—as have Latin American sculptors, painters, authors and architects.

Many Latin American countries are showing signs of being on the verge of a determined drive towards real democracy for the first time. This must, if it succeeds, transform the whole economy of the region. The great gulf between rich and poor and the absence of a middle class has, in the past, meant that only the rich had enough education and power to rule. Now, as the creeping tide of the new democracy begins to spread, a middle class will begin to emerge, providing new rulers who are both closer to the poor and able to transform the industrial and agricultural development of the whole area.

COUNTRIES OF LATIN AMERICA

1 ARGENTINA	13 GUYANA
2 BARBADOS	14 HAITI
3 BOLIVIA	15 HONDURAS
4 BRAZIL	16 JAMAICA
5 CHILE	17 MEXICO
6 COLOMBIA	18 NICARAGUA
7 COSTA RICA	19 PANAMA
8 CUBA	20 PARAGUAY
9 DOMINICAN REPUBLIC	21 PERU
10 ECUADOR	22 TRINIDAD & TOBAGO
11 EL SALVADOR	23 URUGUAY
12 GUATEMALA	24 VENEZUELA

BRAZIL*
Republic
South America
Area: 3,286,000 sq. miles

Pop: 84,679,000. **Land use %:** forest and woodland 46; waste 36; meadow and pasture 16; cultivated 2. **Occupations:** agriculture (coffee, oranges, sugar), stock raising, industry, professions, commerce. **Industries:** iron and steel, textiles, chemicals. **Capital:** Brasilia (300,000).

CHILE*
Republic
South America
Area: 286,000 sq. miles

Pop: 9,200,000. **Land use %:** waste 61; forest 22; grassland 9; cultivated 8. **Occupations:** agriculture, fishing, manufacturing, mining, government services. **Industries:** metal refining, chemicals, petroleum, textiles, foodstuffs, consumer goods. **Capital:** Santiago (2,184,000).

COLOMBIA*
Republic
Northern South America
Area: 455,000 sq. miles

Pop: 18,700,000. **Land use %:** forest 63; grassland 23; waste 12; cultivated 2. **Occupations:** agriculture, mining. **Industries:** textiles, mining, iron, cement. **Capital:** Bogotá (1,406,000).

COSTA RICA*
Republic
Middle America
Area: 20,000 sq. miles

Pop: 1,486,000. **Land use %:** forest 78; cultivated 15; grassland 4; waste 3. **Occupations:** agriculture, mining. **Capital:** San José (186,000).

CUBA*
Republic
Island, Middle America
Area: 44,000 sq. miles

Pop: 7,833,000. **Land use %:** grassland 34; forest 26; waste 23; cultivated 17. **Occupations:** agriculture, manufacturing, commerce, services. **Industries:** tobacco, petroleum, handicrafts, sugar refining. **Capital:** Havana (788,000).

DOMINICAN REPUBLIC*
Republic
W. Indies
Area: 19,000 square miles

Pop: 3,750,000. **Land use %:** forest 69; cultivated 14; grassland 12; waste 5. **Occupations:** subsistence and plantation agriculture, mining. **Industries:** sugar refining, textiles. **Capital:** Santo Domingo (529,000)

ECUADOR*
Republic
West South America
Area: 116,000 sq. miles

Pop: 5,326,000. **Land use %:** forest 55; waste 28; cultivated 11; grassland 6. **Occupations:** subsistence and plantation agriculture, forestry, mining. **Industries:** petroleum, textiles. **Capital:** Quito (510,000).

ARGENTINA*
Republic
S.E. South America
Area: 1,080,000 sq. miles

Pop: 22,700,000. **Land use %:** cultivated 11; permanent meadow and pasture 41; forest and woodland 17; wasteland 31. **Occupations:** stock raising and crop production. **Industries:** meat packing, flour milling, sugar refining, textiles. **Capital:** Buenos Aires (3,000,000; urban area, 6,800,000).

BARBADOS* †
Constitutional Monarchy
Caribbean Sea
Area: 166 sq. miles

Pop: 246,000. **Land use:** cultivated (over 50%), forest, waste. **Occupations:** agriculture (sugar), fishing, construction, manufacturing. **Industries:** foodstuffs, rum production. **Capital:** Bridgetown (94,000).

BOLIVIA*
Republic
W. Central South America
Area: 415,000 sq. miles

Pop: 4,330,000. **Land use %:** waste 55; forest and woodland 44; cultivated 1. **Occupations:** subsistence farming. **Industries:** mining. **Capital:** Sucre (58,000). **Seat of government:** La Paz (461,000).

144

EL SALVADOR*
Republic
Middle America
Area: 8,000 sq. miles

Pop: 3,370,000. **Land use %:** forest 58; waste 24; cultivated 13; grassland 5. **Occupations:** subsistence and plantation agriculture, mining. **Industries:** petroleum, textiles. **Capital:** San Salvador (248,000).

GUATEMALÁ*
Republic
Middle America
Area: 42,000 sq. miles

Pop: 4,575,000. **Land use %:** forest 66; waste 15; cultivated 14; grassland 5. **Occupations:** agriculture (subsistence and plantation). **Industries:** Cement, textiles, consumer goods. **Capital:** Guatemala City (570,000).

GUYANA* †
Constitutional Monarchy
N.E. South America
Area: 83,000 sq. miles

Pop: 662,000. **Land use:** mostly natural forests, cultivated in coastal regions. **Occupations:** agriculture, public services, mining (gold, diamonds, bauxite). **Capital:** Georgetown (188,000).

HAITI*
Republic
W. Indies
Area: 11,000 sq. miles

Pop: 4,700,000. **Land use %:** forest 61; waste 22; cultivated 17. **Occupations:** agriculture. **Industries:** processing agricultural crops. **Capital:** Port-au-Prince (250,000).

HONDURAS*
Republic
Middle America
Area: 43,000 sq. miles

Pop: 2,363,000. **Land use %:** forest 63; waste 32; cultivated 4; grassland 1. **Occupations:** agriculture. **Industries:** timber. **Capital:** Tegucigalpa (200,000).

JAMAICA* †
Constitutional Monarchy
W. Indies
Area: 4,000 sq. miles

Pop: 1,860,000. **Land use:** coastal plains, forest on mountain slopes. **Occupations:** agriculture, mining, petroleum, manufacturing. **Industries:** rum and sugar production, mining (bauxite), cement, consumer goods, tourism. **Capital:** Kingston (511,000).

MEXICO*
Republic
N. America
Area: 758,000 sq. miles

Pop: 44,100,000. **Land use %:** grassland 51; forest 32; waste 12; cultivated 5. **Occupations:** agriculture, mining, fishing, commerce, manufacturing. **Industries:** metal refining, petroleum, foodstuffs, machine assembly, consumer goods. **Capital:** Mexico City (4,659,000).

NICARAGUA*
Republic
Middle America
Area: 54,000 sq. miles

Pop: 1,700,000. **Land use %:** waste 50; forest 44; cultivated 5; grassland 1. **Occupations:** agriculture, manufacturing, commerce. **Capital:** Managua (280,000).

PANAMA*
Republic
Middle America
Area: 29,000 sq. miles

Pop: 1,287,000. **Land use %:** forest 86; waste 12; cultivated 2. **Occupations:** agriculture, government services, commerce, manufacturing. **Industries:** consumer goods. **Capital:** Panama City (344,000).

PARAGUAY*
Republic
South America
Area: 157,000 sq. miles

Pop: 2,094,000. **Land use %:** waste 76; forest 20; cultivated 4. **Occupations:** agriculture, stock rearing, industry. **Industries:** processing foodstuffs. **Capital:** Asuncíon (300,000).

PERU*
Republic
South America
Area: 496,000 sq. miles

Pop: 12,012,000. **Land use %:** forest 56; waste 32; grassland 10; cultivated 2. **Occupations:** agriculture, forestry, fishing, manufacturing, mining. **Industries:** mineral refining, consumer goods. **Capital:** Lima (1,716,000).

TRINIDAD & TOBAGO* †
Constitutional Monarchy
W. Indies
Area: 2,000 sq. miles

Pop: 1,000,000. **Land use:** hilly and very fertile. **Occupations:** agriculture, petroleum, forestry, mining (natural asphalt). **Capital:** Port-of-Spain (94,000).

URUGUAY*
Republic
South America
Area: 72,000 sq. miles

Pop: 2,846,000. **Land use %:** grassland 74; waste 15; cultivated 9; forest 2. **Occupations:** stock raising, agriculture. **Industries:** meat packing, textiles, consumer goods. **Capital:** Montevideo (1,200,000).

VENEZUELA*
Republic
South America
Area: 352,000 sq. miles

Pop: 9,189,000. **Land use %:** forest 40; grassland 32; waste 26; cultivated 2. **Occupations:** agriculture, forestry, transportation, mining, manufacturing, commerce. **Industries:** petroleum, textiles, foodstuffs, iron and steel, chemicals. **Capital:** Caracas (1,336,000).

* Member of the United Nations
† Member of the British Commonwealth

Arctic Ocean

Projection: Polar Equidistant
Heights and depths in metres

Scale: 1: 33,700,000

Miles
0   200   400   600   800   1000

0   200   400   600   800   1000   1200   1400
Kilometres

	Ice caps
	10,000 feet (3000 metres)
	6000 feet (1800 metres)
	3000 feet (900 metres)

	1500 feet (450 metres)
	1000 feet (300 metres)
	500 feet (150 mettes)
	Sea level

International boundaries
Major air routes
Major sea routes

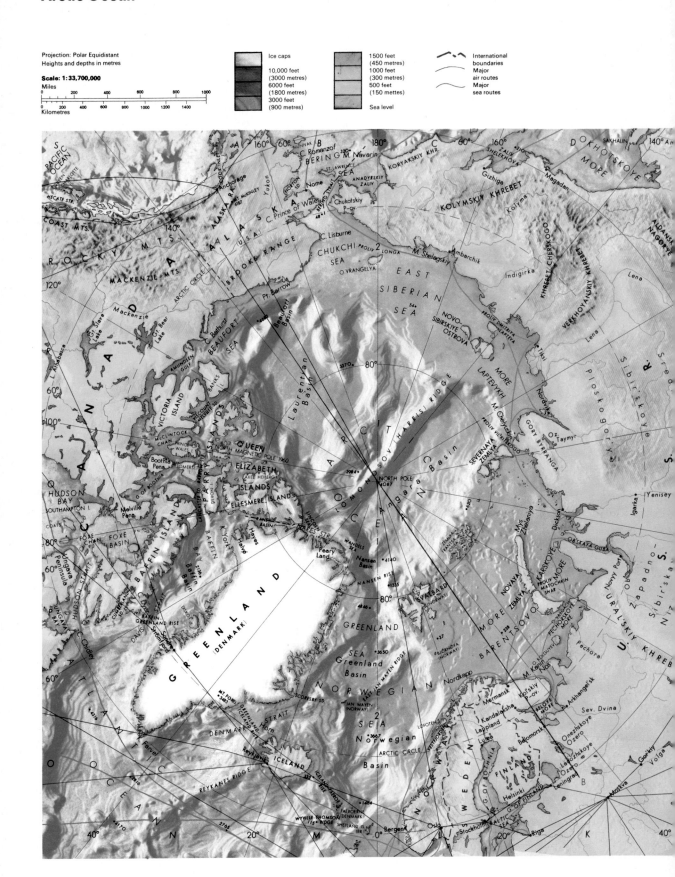

POLAR REGIONS AND THE PACIFIC

It may seem strange to bring together areas as far apart as the Arctic, Antarctic and Oceania; but the two polar regions, crossroads between great continents, are linked by the Pacific Ocean. In the southwest Pacific is Oceania, a region peppered with islands forming stepping stones from Asia to the Americas and ranging in size from tiny atolls to the island continent of Australia.

The Top of the World

From the North Pole every direction is south. From the Pole the Arctic region extends beyond the Arctic Circle (66° 30'N.) to the *tree line*, where forest growth begins. So the Arctic takes in land along the northern coasts of North America and Eurasia, Greenland and islands in the Arctic archipelago.

The heart of the region is the Arctic Ocean, mostly covered all year with pack ice. An ice cap 10,000 feet thick covers most of Greenland. Although there are some mountains—for example, northern Alaska—the flat, monotonous land called *tundra* fringing the Arctic Ocean is most typical. This is really cold desert and, like the hot tropical deserts, it has less than ten inches of rain annually. But rain or snow falls all year instead of in short, sharp bursts, so it is more effective.

The North Pole is not the coldest place in the world. In the Arctic region average July temperatures may be as high as 50°F. The "cold pole" is in northern Siberia (p. 63). Although air temperatures may rise above freezing point during some summer months, the subsoil—called *permafrost*—is always frozen, sometimes to a depth of more than a quarter of a mile. The top soil thaws in summer; melting snow floods the land and the ground becomes waterlogged. But some water runs off into large rivers like the Yenisey (U.S.S.R.) and Mackenzie (Canada), which flow to Arctic seas.

The Arctic has hardly any trees, since the short growing season is cool and the winds are too strong. Only small, low evergreen bushes like bilberry can survive in the acid soils of the tundra, with sedges, cotton grass and moss in wet or peaty ground, lichens in dry areas. In the short summer the landscape is full of color and movement. But in the long winter, with its almost perpetual night, life slows down to a complete stop.

Reindeer (caribou), arctic foxes, musk oxen and

Top: "Hunter with an otter and trap". Soapstone carvings like this reflect the everyday life and experience of the Canadian Eskimo. This unique art form has won interest and respect throughout the world and high prices are now paid for the finest Eskimo carvings.

Above: American submarines *Skate* and *Seadragon* met at the North Pole in 1962. Previously the *Skate* had surfaced at the **Pole** (1959). The first voyage *under* the Pole was also an American achievement—by the U.S.S. *Nautilus* in 1958.

Eskimo fisherman: Eskimos live in the Arctic regions of northeast Asia and North America, from Siberia in the Soviet Union through Alaska and Canada's Northwest Territories to Greenland. There are probably about 50,000 Eskimos in all, and most of them are still hunters, trappers and fishermen.

other migratory animals live in the Arctic. There is abundant marine life. Polar bears and seals share the seas with millions of seabirds.

The Eskimos, Lapps and other native peoples of the Arctic are mostly nomadic. The Eskimos, in Alaska, the Canadian north and Greenland, live by hunting and fishing. Their homes (igloos) are stone and sod houses or tents in summer, and domed snow houses in winter. The Lapps of northern Scandinavia and the Soviet Union live mostly by herding reindeer. Air transportation has increased these peoples' contacts with the modern world and made it easier to help them socially and economically.

The Arctic has important mineral resources. Greenland has lead and cryolite, uranium, beryllium and niobium; Siberia, tin, nickel and diamonds. Coal is mined in Spitsbergen and Canadian oilrigs are working on the Arctic islands off the northeast coast. Both the United States and Canada are building great roads like the Alaska Highway (constructed during World War II) to link the mines and oilfields with the industrial centers farther south. So the economic outlook is promising. The Soviet Union already has a tidal power station at Kislaya Cuba on the White Sea. Some day perhaps the plan to dam the Bering Strait, 56 miles wide, will be a reality.

Many civil airline routes cross the North Pole. It is 1,500 miles shorter from London to Tokyo "over the top" than by the old Mediterranean route. The great powers also maintain military air bases in the Arctic, like the strategically important United States Air Force base at Thule, in western Greenland. Running virtually along the seventieth parallel is North America's chain of defense radar stations, the DEW (Distant Early Warning) line. By far the greater part of the Arctic, however, belongs to the Soviet Union, whose territory stretches from the Norwegian border to the Bering Strait. The North-East Passage is now a regular shipping route for the northern parts of the Soviet Union, served by Arctic weather stations, and powerful icebreakers.

Antarctica

Projection: Polar Equidistant
Heights and depths in metres

Scale: 1:39,200,000

Miles
0   200   400   600   800   1000

Kilometres
0   200   400   600   800   1000   1200   1400   1600   1800

Ice caps
10,000 feet (3000 metres)
6000 feet (1800 metres)
3000 feet (900 metres)

1500 feet (450 metres)
1000 feet (300 metres)
500 feet (150 metres)
Sea level

Towns:
■ over 1,000,000
● under 100,000
· Scientific bases
International boundaries

SOUTH ATLANTIC OCEAN

Argentine Basin

ATLANTIC-ANTARCTIC OR ATLANTIC-INDIAN RIDGE

BOUVETØYA (NORWAY)

PRINCE EDWARD-CROZET RIDGE

MARION I. (SOUTH AFRICA)   PRINCE EDWARD IS.

METEOR SEAMOUNT

Meteor Depth

South Sandwich Trench

SOUTH GEORGIA

SCOTIA SEA

SCOTIA RIDGE

South Sandwich Islands

SHAG ROCKS

TRAVESSAY IS.   VISOKOI IS.   SOUTH SANDWICH ISLANDS
CANDLEMAS IS.   SAUNDERS IS. (MBR)
MONTAGU IS.   BRISTOL

ANTARCTIC CIRCLE

MAUD SEAMOUNT

GUNNERUS BANK

Atlantic-Indian Antarctic Basin

INDIAN OCEAN

FALKLAND ISLANDS
STANLEY   E. FALKLAND
W. FALKLAND

SOUTH ORKNEY ISLANDS
CORONATION

BURDWOOD BANK

DRAKE PASSAGE

SOUTH SHETLAND ISLANDS
ELEPHANT IS.
KING GEORGE IS.
LIVINGSTON IS.
DECEPTION

C. Horn

ARGENTINA   CHILE

TIERRA DEL FUEGO

SOUTH AMERICA

BRITISH ANTARCTIC TERRITORY

GRAHAM LAND

Antarctic Peninsula

PALMER LAND

WEDDELL SEA

Larsen Ice Shelf

Halley Bay

Coats Land

COATS LAND

Maudheim
K. Norwegia

Prinsesse Astrid Kyst   Prinsesse Ragnhild Kyst

Prins Harald Kyst

DRONNING MAUD LAND (NORWAY)

ENDERBY LAND

Mawson
Mac. Robertson Land

Lars Christensen Coast

Amery Ice Shelf

Lambert Glacier

MT. MENZIES

PRYDZ BAY

KING EDWARD VIII GULF

Davis

West Ice Shelf

Princess Elizabeth Land

Kg. Leopold & Qn. Astrid Coast

Wilhelm II Land

Mirny

Queen Mary Land

Shackleton Ice Shelf

KERGUELEN (FR.)

GAUSSBERG RIDGE

BANZARE SEAMOUNT

KERGUELEN-GAUSSBERG RIDGE

GRIBB SEAMOUNT

Recovery Glacier

Filchner Ice Shelf
Shackleton Ice Shelf
Berkner Island

GEORGE VI SOUND

ALEXANDER I.

ELLSWORTH LAND

SENTINEL RA.
VINSON MASSIF

ELLSWORTH MTS.

PENSACOLA MTS.

South Polar Plateau

SOUTH POLE
Amundsen–Scott

AUSTRALIAN ANTARCTIC TERRITORY

Vostok

WILKES LAND

Wilkes

BELLINGSHAUSEN SEA

PETER I. ØYA (NORWAY)

THURSTON ISLAND

C. Flying Fish

Eights Coast

AMUNDSEN SEA

MARIE BYRD LAND

Hollick-Kenyon Plateau

EXECUTIVE COMMITTEE RA.

Getz Ice Shelf

Ruppert Coast

Little America
BAY OF WHALES

ROSS DEPENDENCY (N.Z.)

Ross Ice Shelf

ROOSEVELT I.

King Edward VII Land

MT. EREBUS

C. Crozier
FRANKLIN IS.
Terra Nova Bay

VICTORIA LAND

ROSS SEA

C. Hallett

ADMIRALTY MTS.

Cape Adare

Beardmore Glacier

QUEEN ALEXANDRA RA.

Scott Glacier

Skelton Glacier
McMurdo
McMurdo Sound

TERRE ADÉLIE

Totten Glacier

GEORGE V LAND

Dumont d'Urville

PORPOISE BAY

PACIFIC OCEAN

SOUTHERN OCEAN

SOUTH PACIFIC ANTARCTIC BASIN

PACIFIC-ANTARCTIC RIDGE

South West Pacific Basin

ANTARCTIC CIRCLE

ISELIN BANK

SCOTT

Balleny Basin

BALLENY ISLANDS

MACQUARIE-BALLENY RIDGE

MACQUARIE RISE

Eastern Indian-Antarctic Basin

INDIAN-ANTARCTIC RIDGE

MACQUARIE I. (AUSTR.)

SOUTH TASMANIA RISE

CAMPBELL I. (N.Z.)

NEW ZEALAND PLATEAU

AUCKLAND IS. (N.Z.)

ANTIPODES IS. (N.Z.)

THE SNARES
STEWART I.

BOUNTY IS. (N.Z.)

NEW ZEALAND
Dunedin

CHATHAM RISE

TASMAN SEA

TASMANIA
Hobart
BASS STRAIT

AUSTRALIA
Melbourne

The Antarctic

While the Arctic is an ocean, Antarctica, on the other side of the world, is a huge continent half as large again as the United States. An ice cap, sometimes more than two miles thick, covers the continent but is broken in places by peaks and ranges. There are vast fields of ridged ice, called *sastrugi*, and dangerous crevasses. The ice slowly but continuously works its way towards the coast where massive sections break off and float away as huge flat-topped icebergs. By the Weddell Sea a mountainous peninsula stretches out towards Tierra del Fuego; geologists think this is an extension of the South American Andes. On an island in the Ross Sea is Mount Erebus, Antarctica's only active volcano.

Like the Arctic, Antarctica is in darkness for six months of the year. This and its height make the continent much colder than the Arctic. The surrounding Southern Ocean, mostly covered by pack ice and swept by bitter winds, is the stormiest in the world. It is desolate except for a few islands like South Georgia, the South Shetlands, Heard Island and Bouvet Island. Sea temperature places the boundary of the Antarctic about latitude 50°S., where it is usually warmer than 36°F.

Summer temperatures in Antarctica are always below freezing point and average winter temperatures are the world's lowest, often less than –60°F. In 1960 Vostok, a Russian base, recorded a temperature of –127°F., the coldest ever! Since Antarctica is an area of high pressure, winds blow out from this region, in velocities from 50 miles an hour up to gales of 100 miles an hour. Precipitation, usually snow, is only between four and six inches a year at the South Pole. The snow often comes in "whiteout" blizzards sweeping out from the interior to the continental margins. This kind of climate has been called "the eternal frost".

For the most part Antarctica has no plant life. Some tundra-type vegetation exists on the fringes of the Antarctic Peninsula. But geologists have found fossil plant remains that show the region was once much warmer.

The seas are rich in plankton. This includes krill, the small shrimps on which the 100-ton Blue Whale, the world's largest mammal, feeds. So valuable are whale oil and its by-products that fleets come to the Antarctic from all over the world to hunt the Blue and other whales, often ignoring the restrictions

Top: the South Pole. Because the earth wobbles a little as it spins the Pole changes position slightly hour by hour. The path of these changes of position takes the form of a rough circle, shown here marked out by a ring of drums. The ice sheet covering the Pole is 8,300 feet thick.

150

Meeting at the South Pole on January 19, 1958.
Sir Edmund Hillary (center) with Sir Vivian Fuchs
(right) and Rear-Admiral George Dufek, U. S. Navy.

Below: the Palmer or Graham Land Peninsula just inside
the Antarctic Circle. Its mountains are thought to be a
continuation of the South American Andes.
Bottom: an icebreaker in the Antarctic Ocean making her
way through open water in the ice, to the Antarctic mainland.

imposed to prevent extermination. The only other animals are seals, penguins and other marine birds, all dependent on the ocean for their food.

It is doubtful if the Antarctica's mineral resources are workable. There is coal, uranium, iron ore, copper and lead, but all of these would be very costly to work and transport. Some people have suggested that the Antarctic might be a huge natural refrigerator for surplus food storage; others suggest that since few germs can withstand the cold, it might be a world sanatorium.

Antarctica has no native people and will probably never make any great economic contribution to our everyday life. But it is an intensely interesting region to scientists. Their studies include the ice and its influence on the climate of the rest of the world. Since the glaciers in the northern hemisphere are shrinking, scientists want to know if Antarctic glaciers are shrinking too and, if so, what the effects will be on the weather and level of the seas. If all the Antarctic ice were to melt, the water released would flood low-lying cities like New York, Tokyo and London.

No airlines yet route their flights over the South Pole as they do over the North. But if South Polar routes were used, the flying time between Buenos Aires and Melbourne would be halved.

The Antarctic is not owned by any one country. One result of the International Geophysical Year, which ended on December 31 1958, was the important treaty signed by twelve nations in Washington in 1959. The United States, the United Kingdom, Australia, New Zealand, South Africa, the Soviet Union, Norway, France, Argentina, Chile, Belgium and Japan agreed that for 30 years Antarctic should be reserved for free research. Here at least there is peaceful coexistence between nations.

151

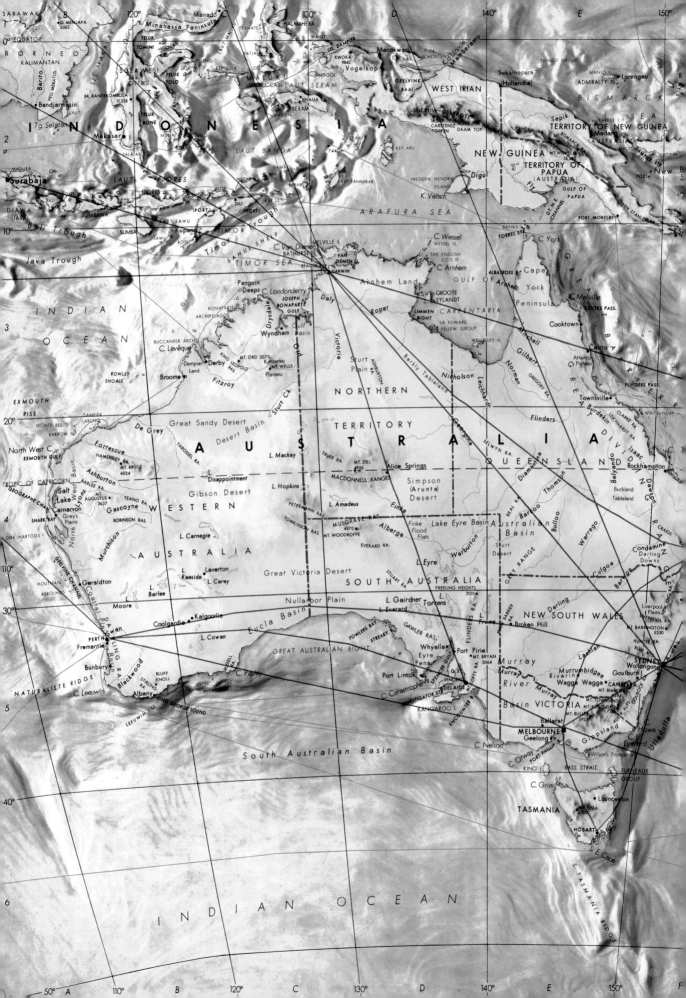

Australasia

Projection: Lambert's Equal Area
Heights in feet depths in metres

Scale: 1:21,800,000

Miles
0   100   200   300   400   500   600

Kilometres
0   100 200 300 400 500 600 700 800 900

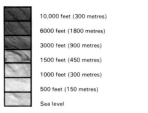

10,000 feet (300 metres)
6000 feet (1800 metres)
3000 feet (900 metres)
1500 feet (450 metres)
1000 feet (300 metres)
500 feet (150 metres)
Sea level

Towns:

■ over 1,000,000
● over   500,000
● over   250,000
• under 250,000

〜〜〜 State boundaries
――― Major air routes
――― Major sea routes

The Pacific Islands

Yam store house in a village in the Trobriand Islands. Administered by Australia, these coral islands lie 150 miles southeast of Papua, New Guinea. The islanders, who are a mixture of Melanesian and Polynesian stock, export mainly pearls and pearl shells.

The Pacific, the world's largest and deepest ocean, is studded with islands. There are more than 30,000 of them, mostly tropical and mostly in the southwest Pacific (Oceania), where high ridges and deep troughs cut the ocean bed. Many are grouped in archipelagos. Some are coral atolls, low and sandy, with lovely lagoons. Canton Island in the Phoenix group, an important staging point on international air routes until the development of long-range jet aircraft, is a typical atoll. Some islands are mountainous and volcanic, deeply covered by fertile soil formed by eroded lava rock, and fringed by mangrove swamps. The Mariana group are formed by the summits of fifteen drowned volcanic mountains.

Since they are mostly within the tropics, the islands have a warm climate. The temperature hardly varies between summer and winter. Many coral islands have little rain and their vegetation is poor. But heavy rain falls on mountainous volcanic islands, like Hawaii, and these are covered with lush vegetation. Tropical jungles in the lowlands sometimes spread up to cover the steep mountainsides.

Although Thor Heyerdahl crossed the Pacific from Peru on his raft *Kon Tiki* to prove that settlers came to the Pacific from South America, most experts still believe that the main migrations came from southern and south-eastern Asia. The three chief divisions of the Pacific islands are named for the migrant peoples who came this way long before Europeans and other "non-Pacific" peoples arrived. *Melanesia*, with more than 370,000 square miles of land, includes Fiji, the Solomon Islands, New Caledonia, the New Hebrides and other islands in the

southwest. The Mariana, Caroline, Gilbert, Marshall and other northwest islands, including Nauru and Wake, form *Micronesia*. The islands of the east and central Pacific within the Hawaii-Easter Island-New Zealand triangle are *Polynesia*. Most of them are the small tops of volcanic mountains, and in places wind and rain have eroded the lava rock to produce rich soils.

Cultures, customs and languages differ from island to island, and sometimes from village to village. The Melanesians, stocky and frizzy-haired, are mostly fishermen and traders. Many are Christians, but others cling to magic and belief in the supernatural. The Micronesians, slight in build, straight-haired and copper skinned, are skillful sailors and fishermen. Most are Christians. The tall, well-built, light-skinned Polynesians have a high cultural level. They too are fishermen, but they are also skilled craftsmen. Their wooden frame houses, thatched with palm or pandanus, are often built on raised stones or earth to help keep them dry during the rainy season. The Hawaiians, Maoris, Samoans, Tahitians and Tongans are the chief groups of Polynesia.

In some Pacific islands comparative newcomers have become prominent. Fiji, for example, now has more Indians than Fijians. Many Japanese, Filipinos and Chinese live in Hawaii, whose capital and chief port, Honolulu, is the only large city in the islands.

The coconut palm, a valuable basic source of food, clothing and shelter, grows everywhere. It has been called "the trademark of the Pacific", and

provides many islands with their only commercial product—copra. The islands grow food crops, including yams, taros, breadfruit, sweet potatoes, bananas and cassava for local consumption; and some islands produce food on a commercial scale. Hawaii is known for its sugar-cane and pineapples. Both are also grown in Fiji, along with rice and cacao. New Caledonia has large coffee plantations. Western Samoa exports cocoa.

Mineral resources are limited and scattered. New Caledonia is rich in nickel, chrome, iron ore and manganese. Here, too, silver, gold, cobalt, lead and copper have been mined intermittently. There are gold mines in Fiji. Large quantities of phosphate, an essential fertilizer, come from Nauru and Ocean islands.

The seclusion of the Pacific from the mainstream of new ideas, the isolation of the island communities one from another, the limited natural resources and shortages of land and manpower have held back the progress of the islands. In most cases their future still rests with Western countries like Australia, Britain, France, New Zealand and the United States. But some of the islands have made political progress. Hawaii became the 50th state of the Union in 1959. Western Samoa became self-governing in 1962 but remained within the Commonwealth of Nations. Tiny Nauru became independent in 1968. Economic progress, however, still requires the development of both industry and trade—a task in which the two most highly developed countries of Oceania, Australia and New Zealand, can take an important part.

Top: Waikiki Beach, Honolulu, the capital and chief port of the state of Hawaii. The city is on the island of Oahu.
Below: a christening feast in Tonga. Feelings of kinship are very strong among Polynesian people and it is not unusual for as many as 200 people to attend a feast like this.

Australasia

The smallest continent, and the only continent which is one country, is Australia. Most of the continent is rolling plain or low plateau, broken in the northwest and center by more rugged country. Running down the east coast behind the narrow coastal plain is the Great Dividing Range, a watershed chain of tablelands and mountains culminating in the Australian Alps and Mount Kosciusko (7,316 ft.), Australia's highest peak. These highlands reappear in Tasmania, Australia's offshore state. Another feature of the east coast is the Great Barrier Reef, 1,250 miles long.

The northern third of Australia lies in the tropics. The climate of the whole continent is generally warm and dry. The farther inland you go, the drier it becomes. Rainfall is heaviest along the north coast east of Darwin, along the east and southeast coasts, and in the southwest around Perth. Most of the western two thirds of Australia is stony desert. The best pastures and farmlands are in the warm, moist southeast. Here the Murray River, with the Darling, Murrumbidgee and other tributaries, forms Australia's chief river system. Vast areas rely on artesian well water. The Great Artesian Basin, covering most of Queensland and parts of South Wales, South Australia and the Northern Territory, is probably the world's largest source of artesian water. Dams and irrigation have helped solve water problems. The most ambitious project, the Snowy Mountains scheme, provides both irrigation and hydroelectric power.

Australia is more than ten times the size of Texas. But its population is comparatively small—nearly 12 million—and more than half lives in the state capitals. Sydney, capital of New South Wales and Australia's largest city, has a population of nearly 2 ½ million. Melbourne, capital of Victoria, has more than 2 million inhabitants.

Most Australians are of British origin. But since World War II about one million other Europeans have migrated there. The Australian Aborigines still live their "Stone Age" nomadic life in the remoter parts of the continent.

More than a quarter of the world's wool comes from Australia, which is also a major producer of wheat, beef and dairy cattle, sugar-cane and fruits. Mineral resources include gold, lead, silver, zinc, copper, coal, uranium and bauxite. There is some commercial petroleum production in Queensland and natural gas has been found in Papua. The development of these resources and British, Canadian and American investment have made Australia a highly industrialized country, now producing a lot of the manufactures she used to import.

Ayers Rock, a vast sandstone monolith between the George Gill and Musgrave Ranges in the southwest of the Northern Territory, Australia. It is more than one and a half miles long, a mile wide and 1,100 feet high. Its caves contain aboriginal rock paintings.

Top: Mission Bay, a popular beach of Auckland, New Zealand. With its suburbs Auckland is the largest city in New Zealand, and a leading port and commercial center of the North Island. It stands on the narrow isthmus between the Waitemata and Manukau harbors.

Right: gum trees and sheep near Berrivale, New South Wales, Australia. Eucalyptus or gum trees are characteristic of Australia. Below: Brisbane, the capital and chief port of Queensland, Australia, straddles Brisbane River about 18 miles from the sea.

Geologists think Australia was once part of a much larger land mass. About 50 million years ago the land bridge between Australia and Asia disappeared. One result was that Australian wildlife developed independently and now includes many unique species; the duckbilled platypus, the flightless emu and marsupials (pouched animals) like the kangaroo.

Across the Tasman Sea about 1,200 miles southeast of Australia is New Zealand. About two-thirds of the population (2,712,000) live in the fertile, volcanic North Island, whose centers are Auckland and Wellington, the capital. The South Island, long and narrow, is dominated by the Southern Alps. Christchurch is its largest city.

Most New Zealanders are of British stock, but there are about 200,000 Maoris, mostly on the North Island. Like Australia, New Zealand is an important agricultural producer (mutton, dairy produce and wool). There are extensive forests. Mineral resources include gold, coal, some petroleum and natural gas, and iron sands which may become the basis of a small iron and steel industry. Hydroelectric schemes on the Waikato and other rivers and natural steam provide ample power.

Pacific Ocean

Projection: Mercator

Heights and depths in metres

Scale: 1 : 56,800,000 equatorial scale

Miles
0   500   1000   1500

Kilometres
0   500   1000   1500   2000

10,000 feet (3000 metres)
6000 feet (1800 metres)
3000 feet (900 metres)
1500 feet (450 metres)

1000 feet (300 metres)
500 feet (150 metres)
Sea level

International boundaries
Major air routes
Major sea routes

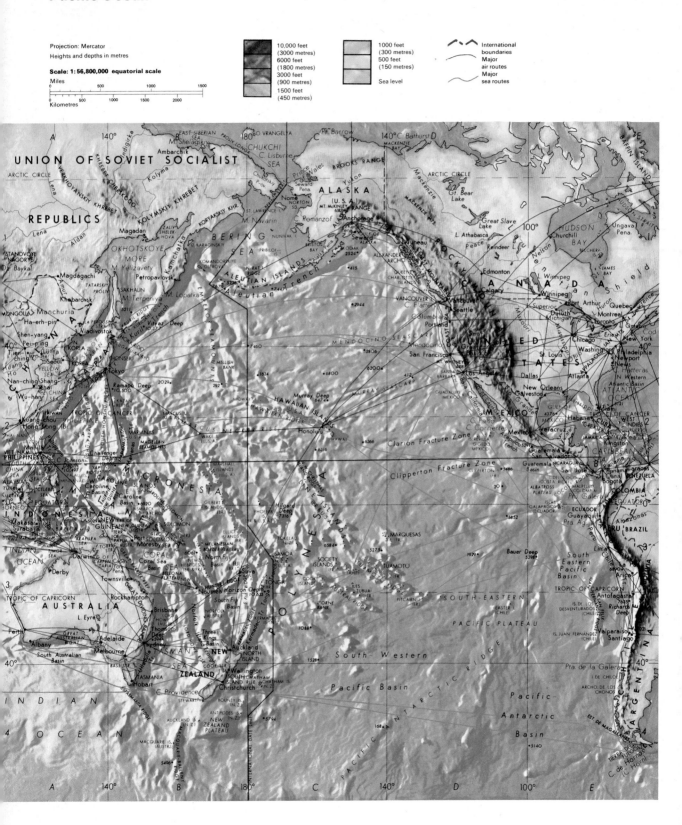

Sunset at Bora-Bora, one of the Leeward Islands in French Polynesia. The island is almost completely encircled by a coral reef. Within the lagoon is the island of Tupua. During World War II Bora-Bora was an American air and naval base.

Thatching a hut in Fiji, a British colony in the west Pacific. Fiji consists of about 320 islands, some rugged and volcanic, others just coral atolls. Only about a hundred of the islands are inhabited. Suva, the chief town, is on Viti Levu, the largest of the group. Sugar is Fiji's most valuable export, followed by coconut oil, gold, copra and bananas. Nadi airport is an important staging point on trans-Pacific air routes.

COUNTRIES OF OCEANIA

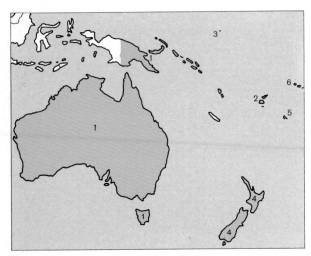

1 AUSTRALIA
2 FIJI
3 NAURU

4 NEW ZEALAND
5 TONGA
6 WESTERN SAMOA

AUSTRALIA* †
Constitutional Monarchy
S. Pacific
Area: 2,968,000 sq. miles

Pop: 11,651,000. **Land use %:** cultivated 1; meadow and pasture 48; forest and woodland 4; waste 47. **Occupations:** manufacturing, agriculture and forestry, commerce, mining. **Industries:** textiles, iron and steel, manufacturing, forestry, commerce, mining. **Federal Capital:** Canberra (100,000). **State capitals** (with population): Sydney (New South Wales) 2,485,000; Melbourne (Victoria) 2,108,000; Brisbane (Queensland) 778,000; Adelaide (South Australia) 726,000; Perth (Western Australia) 558,000; Hobart (Tasmania) 53,000. **Territories:** The Northern Territory; Papua and New Guinea; Norfolk Island; Ashmore and Cartier Islands; Heard and McDonald Islands; Cocos-Keeling Islands; Christmas Island; Australian Antarctic Territory.

FIJI
U.K. Colony
S. Central Pacific
Area: 7,000 sq. miles

Pop: 477,000. **Land use %:** forest 52; waste 37; cultivated 8; grassland 2. **Occupations:** agriculture, manufacturing, commerce. **Industries:** sugar refining, timber. **Capital:** Suva (54,000).

NAURU †
Republic
S. Pacific
Area: 8½ sq. miles

Pop: 7,000. **Occupations:** phosphate production. **Capital:** Nauru.

NEW ZEALAND* †
Constitutional Monarchy
S. Pacific
Area: 104,000 sq. miles

Pop: 2,712,000. **Land use %:** grassland 46; forest 25; waste 25; cultivated 4. **Occupations:** manufacturing, agriculture, forestry, commerce, government service. **Industries:** timber, processing agricultural products, coal, chemicals, consumer goods. **Capital:** Wellington (282,000). **Islands and Territories:** Cook Islands (internally self governing); Ross Dependency (Antarctica).

TONGA
U.K.-protected Kingdom
S. Central Pacific
Area: 270 sq. miles

Pop: 74,000. **Land use:** forested, but widely cultivated. **Occupations:** subsistence farming, fishing. **Capital:** Nukualofa (9,000).

WESTERN SAMOA †
Independent State
Central Pacific
Area: 1,000 sq. miles

Pop: 132,000. **Land use;** mountainous, but well cultivated. **Occupations:** subsistence and plantation farming. **Capital:** Apia (22,000).

* Member of the United Nations
† Member of the British Commonwealth

Picture credits
Aerofilms Ltd., 12(BR), 23(B); Aeroservice Corporation 107(T); Associated Press 27; ATP Zürich 81 (BL); Australian News & Information Bureau 154 (BL); Barnabys Australia Colour Agency 157(C); Elizabeth Bott 155(B); British Crown copyright reserved 85(B), 159(B); British Steel Corporation 21(L); Photo courtesy of British Travel Association 10; Camera Press 70(T), 72(T); photo Jacques Berque 53(B); Canadian Pacific photograph 121(B); J. Allan Cash 13, 17(TR), 23(T), 33(T), 34(T), 51(T), 84(T), 88(BL), 91(T), 92(B), 93, 104(TL), 108–9(T), 108(B), 109(B), 125(TL), 143(B), 157(BR); *China Pictorial* 81(TR), 88(B); Civici Musei Veneziani d'Arte e di Storia 37(L); Harrison Church 37(BR); Conzett & Huber, Zürich 39(B); Conzett & Huber, Zürich, photo Anita Niesz 22(B); C.S. Services Limited 89(T); Hans Erni 90; Ethiopian Tourist Organization (Bernheim) 53(T); FAO photo 83(B); Fiat, Turin 37(TR); Courtesy of Finnish Travel Association 19(T); Courtesy of French Government Tourist Office, London 36(TL); Fry, Drew & Partners, Architects, London 55(B); Ewing Galloway 126; Ewing Galloway from Popperfoto 98(TL); Geographical Projects 24–25, 28–29, 42–43, 47, 56–61, 86–87, 95–97, 101–103, 126–127, 136–137, 144–146, 149, 152–153, 158; Françoise Girard 154; Grand Union Co. 123(B); Guozi Shudian, Peking 80(TR); E. Haeberlin 52(R); Dr. Toni Hagen 76(B); Sonia Halliday 68(TL); Reproduced by permission of Her Britannic Majesty's Postmaster General 55(C); Hudson's Bay Company 148(T); Cliché IGN 16; Infoplan 155(TR); Interfoto MTI. 71(T); Istituto Geografico De Agostini di Novara 18(B); Japan National Tourist Organization 83; Japanese Information Centre, London 82(T); Jones and Laughlin Steel Corp., Pittsburgh 106(TL); Pall Jonsson 12(BL); Sara Leighton 159(T); Herbert List 132(BR); Photo Ludwig, Hamburg 30; Terence McNally 48–49(B); Magnum Photos, Ansel Adams 133(B); Werner Bischof 22(T); Rene Burri 139(T); Henri Cartier-Bresson 70(B); Elliott Erwitt 72(T); Sergio Larrain 130, 135(B), 138(T); Marc Riboud 48–49(C), 51(B), 80(CL); Photo Dr. T. A. Margerison 50(B); Paul Henry Mellinghaus, München 52(L); Josef Muench, F.P.S.A. 115(B); David Muench 121(T); National Aeronautics and Space Administration 2–3; National Film Board of Canada 98(TR) (B), 100, 106(TR), 116(T) (B), 117; Courtesy of Netherlands National Tourist Office (ANVV) 14(R); Novosti Press Agency 68(TR), 69(TL); Official U.S. Navy photo 148(C); Pan-Am, 134; P.A.-Reuter 34(B), 79(T); Picturepoint, London 17(B), 38–39(C), 40, 41, 44, 77(T), 79(B), 82(BL), 92(TL), 95(B), 104(BL), 105, 107(B), 112(TL), 113, 133(T), 156, 157(TL); Polar Photos 150–151(C); Foto Pontis 74; photo Herzog 38–39(T); Popperfoto 15(B), 33(B), 48–49(T), 77(B), 78(B), 100 (TL), 139(B); Rapho-Guillumette, photo William W. Bacon 148(B); Photo P. Millet – *Réalités* 36(R); Bernard Richardson 12(TL), 14(TL), 17(TL), 26(T), 54, 66, 76(T), 88(T), 114(TL), 132; Photo Robert Yarnall Richie 55(T); Fulvio Roiter 32, 35(T), 135(T), 141(TR), 142; Courtesy Salt Lake Area Chamber of Commerce 114(B); Emil Schulthess 94, 150–151(B); Shell/BP International photographs 46, 79(T); A Shell photograph 143(T); Photo Glen Peterson from Shostal 123(T); Society for Cultural Relations with U.S.S.R., London 67(TR), 69(TR), 71(B); Sony Camera Corporation, Tokyo 89(C); *Soviet Union* 65(BL), 69(TL); Staatliche Antikensammlungen und Glyptothek, München 35(B); Stern Archive 15(T), 67(TL); The Swedish Institute for Cultural Relations 21(TR); Swissair, cover, 78(T), 85(T), 91(BL) (BR), 118(T), 141(TL); Syndication International Ltd. 120(T); Tate & Lyle Refineries Limited 138(B); The Farm Quarterly, 119; Photo Thiele 47,62; Photo Leonard McCombe © Time Inc. 140(L); Trans-Antarctic Expedition 151(TR); Courtesy United States Information Service, London 92(TR), 111, 112(BL), 115(T), 119(T), 125(B), 150–151(T); Photos by USDA 118(C) (B); Jean Verbruggen: *Sabena Review* 122; Photo Voks, Berne 65(TL) (TR) (BR); Wideroe's Flyveselskap 19(B)
In a work of this nature, necessarily dependent upon illustrations reproduced from a multitude of sources all over the world, it is often difficult, and sometimes impossible, to ascertain whether or not a particular illustration is in copyright, and if it is, who is the owner. If we have unwittingly infringed copyright in any picture or photograph reproduced in this book, we tender our sincere apologies and will be glad of the opportunity, upon being satisfied as to the owner's title, to pay an appropriate fee as if we had been able to obtain prior permission.